D0896416

By the author of
"The Star-Borne — A Remembrance for the
Awakened Ones" and
"Invoking Your Celestial Guardians."

The Legend of Altazar

A FRAGMENT OF THE TRUE HISTORY OF PLANET EARTH

BY
THE HERMIT OF THE CRYSTAL MOUNTAIN

Star-Borne Unlimited
Route 7 Box 191B
Charlottesville, VA 22901

First Edition published April 1987
Fourth Edition published November 1990

ISBN #1-878246-02-X

Cover Illustration from the vision of the
        Hermit of the Crystal Mountain
Sky-Maker: Sherie Lewis
Star-Maker: Gary Lee Applegate

Typesetting: Elara Zacandra

Printed in the United States of America

DEDICATED TO THE OG-MIN
AND TO ALL CONSCIOUS BEINGS
WHO HAVE SERVED AMONG US
SINCE THE BEGINNING OF TIME.

Now is the time
Whereupon we fit
The crystal-tipped arrows
Into our flexible bows
Strung with the Light of Clarity.

They are set loose
Within the world of men,
We are set free
To return to our starry homes,
Completed—at last.

THERE SHALL BE NO-DOWN / NO-RETURN

And To Nova
Who Stood Beside Me,
Dried My Tears,
And Understood.

INTRODUCTION

First I must admit that I had no intention of writing a book. I was happily living a quiet life as a hermit in the mountains. I truly enjoyed the Silence. I assumed that I had already given what service I could.

Then this story came. This story came and would not let me go. At first I tried my best to get it out of my mind. Yet, it persisted. Finally, I thought that if I wrote it down, it would release me. Besides, surely, I could finish the story in about five pages. Well, as you can see, I was tricked as we so often are when spirit calls us to do something.

So I set to work on my short story, and before I knew it, this persistent tale turned into a book! I wasn't totally pleased about this discovery, as I had *no* intention of writing a book. Still, try as I might, I could not set it aside.

Back at the beginning when I realized that a portion of this story took place in Lemuria, I was perplexed as well. I knew nothing of Lemuria, so how could I be expected to write about it? Besides, I was told to use no reference works. In order to solve this severe dilemma of writing a story which I did not want to write, set in places of which I had no conscious recall, I was forced to tap into heretofore unused parts of myself. I would simply sit quietly with a blank pad of paper in hand, (*and with a blank mind, I might add,*) and wait until I could *see* the story. Then I wrote down what I saw. This process was indeed full of constant surprises. Characters disappeared whom I had grown quite fond of, while new ones were introduced whom I had not expected.

Somewhere within this lengthy process, I began to enjoy the experience of being the scribe for the Hermit of the Crystal Mountain. So you see, although I was initially resistant to becoming part of this process, it must now be stated that I am most grateful for having been chosen to serve this task. Life is always full of strange and unexpected surprises, is it not?

I feel that the messages and triggers within THE LEGEND OF ALTAZAR are extremely timely and important. So many of us have been dangling on the brink between breakdown and breakthrough. We have experienced the death and transformation of so many old habits and out-dated forms. We are truly the pioneers, the wayshowers into the future and into the Unknown. Yet, it certainly has not been easy for us to reach this point. Often it has seemed as if we were tested and blocked at every turn. And still we continue on, still we endure, doing our utmost to serve our Higher Purpose.

Well, the old mode of struggle and sorrow is changing. Now the only limitations that hinder us are the ones that we have placed there ourselves and keep in position by believing in their reality. We are entirely free to step into the beautiful state of grace, joy and abundance that are our true birthrights & heritage. This I know for certain.

Mankind is currently being aided by the Higher Realms on a scale never before experienced. But we would do well to remember, that not only are we being helped from on high, *we are the help from on high!*

THE LEGEND OF ALTAZAR – is *your* story. Altazar, Diandra, Solana and all the others whom you shall soon meet exist within each one of you. They are the Master Patterns for humanity. It is my fervent desire that by reading this humble story you shall be inspired to bring them forth within you to fulfill their final duty.

Your greatest initiation is unfolding. The doorway stands open before you. You are hereby handed the Golden Key with which to unlock your Higher Purpose. The need for this is great indeed, for the time is now. Please dear readers, come forth, be who you are and unsheath your crystal-tipped arrows.

And may this crystal-tipped arrow, the one which I have thus sent forth from my bow, find its mark within your heart and within your destiny pattern that it may awaken your remembrance.

With Love and Blessings,

Solara

A BRIEF CHAPTER SUMMARY OF
THE LEGEND OF ALTAZAR

I CANNOT BE MORE THAN I AM.

I CANNOT BE LESS THAN I AM.

BUT I MUST BE THAT I AM.

CHAPTER ONE:
THE HIGH KING
& THE HIGH PRIESTESS

Once upon a time in the long lost ago known as the Golden Age, there lived a mighty king named Altazar. He was not simply an ordinary king, nor even a great king, but was a true monarch of the sort that the world has not seen since that distant age. For his very name, Altazar, meant High King, and that he truly was.

Altazar ruled over a large island off the coast of what is now called Australia, part of the ancient continent of Lemuria. His was an enlightened and noble rule. He was much beloved by his people who did indeed flourish under his care as did the animals, the birds, the very trees, flowers and rocks of his kingdom. Possibly this was due in part to the fact that Altazar did not consider himself separate from anyone or anything on his large island. He cared for everything as deeply as he cared for himself, seeing the spark of the Creator in all. Part of his magic was his ability to call forth the very best from not only his people who were truly devoted to him, but also from his plants, which the legend saith, produced incredible yields of fruits and vegetables, while his flowers bloomed in ever more magnificent displays. Even the animals were peaceable with each other and showed no fear of the humans. His island, Arnahem, was a true paradise indeed.

When it came time for Altazar to marry, a search throughout the Lemurian Empire commenced; but alas, no bride who was his equal could be found. No woman was in possession of such grace, virtue and wisdom to be a worthy mate of the High King. Accordingly, the High Priests of this land had but one choice. They gathered together at the High Temple of Tana on the main land mass and through the crystal that had been given to them at the Beginning, they sent a message telepathically to the High Priests of the Great Continent of Atlantis far across the world, asking for a suitable bride to be sent for Altazar.

In faraway Atlantis, the message was received with utmost respect. The Brotherhood of the Seven met in council and pondered well the request. Alorah, the Highest Priestess of the Temple of Creative Healing Wisdom, (ORALIN), was summoned. She was asked whom she would choose to unite these two great civilizations through marriage. Withdrawing her essence to the Cave Heavens far, far away—to that place of all knowing, she saw the face of one of her High Priestesses appear. It was the beautiful Diandra. Ah yes, it was she. Diandra of the long cascading blond hair, of the wide-set, all-seeing blue eyes, Diandra with the finely chiselled cheekbones. Yes, it was Diandra—holder of the Seven Knots of Healing Wisdom.

Then, she too was summoned and told of her assignment and she readily agreed to go. Of course, Diandra felt a great sadness in her heart at leaving her homeland and her people, especially for leaving her work in the Temple of

Oralin. She worked closely with many of the lesser initiates, leading them through the doorways that go to the inner sanctums. But her training was completed to such a high level, seven knots, that she could function well on her own. She had her telepathic link with her Masters who held the key that unlocks the magnetic grid. This grid encircles the Master Grid whereupon she could tap into the Source.

Diandra returned with Alorah to the temple where she began rigorous fasting, purifications, and irradiations with different crystalline energies to complete her preparations for her journey.

On the appointed morning, the seven members of the Brotherhood of the Seven presented themselves at the portals of her temple. Diandra appeared clad in a flowing, luminescent gown of white. Around her waist was the deep purple sash of the initiates of the Temple of Oralin, tied with seven knots. She bowed to the Seven as they bowed to her; then they led her through the quiet white streets of Atlantis past the gleaming white domed temples, past the Tower of Truth, past the fountain whose Waters of Clarity she would drink no more, to that section of the city that was forbidden to all—unless you be one of the Makers or possessed nine knots on your belt. *(Nine knots were had by very few, very few indeed. But there were whispers that somewhere in Atlantis were ones who wore eleven knots. No one had ever seen these ones, if indeed they existed at all.)*

As they came to this highest of places, the first of the Seven halted at a gleaming golden gate barring their path. The thin and delicate spires glowed brilliantly in the sunlight. Bringing forth a crystal from his robe, he pointed it at the gate and muttered words that sounded like—

"Aztlan-Inra." The gate immediately disappeared and our party of eight walked through. After they had passed by, Diandra glanced back quickly and saw the gate, once again firmly in position.

Ahead of her was a high hill dotted with strange structures, mainly composed of various geometric shapes. They proceeded up a steep and winding path until it forked, whereupon they chose the left one which was much narrower. As soon as they turned onto this seldom used path, Diandra noticed a change in the quality of light. Everything appeared to have a blueish tinge to it. As they continued, the hue became even stronger until it turned a deep cobalt. There was an aura of highly charged electrical currents just off the path on both sides. Then the path forked once again and they turned to the right this time. Diandra, despite her training and well developed sense of control, could not help feeling excited and even a bit frightened. The power that was available here was awesome indeed. Taking a deep breath, she consciously relaxed her being and continued on.

Suddenly the path ended abruptly at a solid stone wall made of a highly polished marble. The cobalt air had transmuted into deepest indigo. It was intense. Diandra had trouble controlling her breathing.

The first of the Seven whispered something that sounded like—*"Aztlan-Egri"* and walked into the wall and disappeared! The others followed one by one and also disappeared from sight. Diandra's eyes widened with surprise; she swallowed to pull herself together, and summoning her full authority, she also walked into the wall and appeared to vanish.

They were inside a large chamber. The top of the room

was capped by a glass-like pyramid. *(This pyramid was really made of a man-made crystal composed elsewhere on this secret hill.)* In the center of the room under the apex of the crystal pyramid was a smaller three-sided pyramid also made of crystal. Inside it stood a small pedestal fashioned out of a huge piece of smoky quartz.

The Elder of the Seven motioned for Diandra to stand before him. Then in the secret gesture of high initiates, he placed both of his hands palms down over her two outstretched hands—palms up, but not touching. The transmission was made.

Then Diandra knew. She saw it all clearly. She saw the beginning and the end. She saw it all with crystal clarity, sensing that this was the commencement of her real Purpose. All of her training had been leading up to this moment. She saw too, Altazar, seeing his handsomeness, his nobility, his impeccable virtue. Then she realized that he also was a high initiate who had obtained eight knots in secret training in her very own city and no one had even known that he had been here. Her heart filled with love for him—for the fineness of his being, for his compassion, for the experiences that they would share together. And then she saw more. She saw his downfall, how although he would be spared, he would suffer the most. How he would . . . Oh no! Tears streamed down her face and she could look no more. "Oh, my poor beloved Altazar! If you could but change your destiny. My heart breaks for you."

Slowly remembering where she was, Diandra looked up at the Seven standing there so patiently, so lovingly, gazing at her with tears in their eyes too. Suddenly it struck her how magnificent were the dedication and wisdom of the Brotherhood of the Seven. They were the keepers of such heavy responsibilities; yet they still maintained impeccable compassion. She remembered the saying etched in stone above the doorway to one of the temples, *"Power Brings With It Responsibility."* Looking at the Seven's well-worn faces, she saw that they had not fully transmuted all of the burdens that they carried so that Atlantis might thrive and carry out its Plan.

The image of the High Priestess Alorah flashed through her mind. She saw her dressed in her white and blue ceremonial robes with the breastplate containing what appeared to be real twinkling tiny stars. Alorah was known to be not from this planet and maintained her contact with her family of starry beings far, far away. Diandra thanked her silently for her teachings and thought fondly of her family of friends in the temples.

"I am leaving this all. I am leaving my homeland, my people, and will, most likely, never return," she thought as twinges of sadness coursed through her. Then she remembered Altazar and felt his great need for her. This steadied her. She was ready.

The first of the Seven reached down and tied an eighth knot in her sash. "Farewell, daughter," he said. *(If it could but be told, you might know that he really was her father, but that would make another story.)* He gestured for Diandra to enter the small crystal pyramid and seat herself upon the smoky quartz.

*** *** ***

And thus did our fair Diandra leave Atlantis and go to the land of Altazar. And this I know for certain. Because in some form or another, I was there.

CHAPTER TWO:
THE ENCOUNTER

Diandra opened her eyes and was immediately hit with a piercing orange light. She closed them again and dared not move. Where was she? Was she in Atlantis or was she in Arnahem? She sat very still, feeling the subtle energy around her as she had been trained to do—searching for clues.

Suddenly the tone of a gong shattered the silence with a prolonged fullness of deep resonance. She waited until the hypnotic sound had almost totally faded from her memory. Then opening those large clear eyes of hers, she stood up and walked forward. She could see nothing but the brightest of orange lights and yet our brave Diandra walked forward using her finely developed vibrational senses.

"Welcome, my Queen," proclaimed a deep voice from the stillness. Diandra stepped through the intense orange light into a circular room bathed in the vibrant green of vitality and growth. There was the sound of running water, possibly a fountain somewhere. And there he was, Altazar, standing in front of her, smiling warmly. He was even stronger, more handsome, more alive, than she had ever imagined. Tall with dark hair tinged with grey, Altazar had a full beard which made his dark brown eyes stand out dramatically. They flashed with strength, love and humour.

Altazar was clad, or partially clad, in a brown cloth wrapped around his waist which fell below his knees. This shimmered when he moved, changing colors ever so slightly as a pattern of delicate tropical flowers emerged. His chest was bare and covered with hair, something that she had rarely observed in Atlantis. A golden dagger hung from a sash around his waist and a rough cut diamond set in gold encircled his neck. Altazar's head was wrapped in a white turban-like covering from which protruded iridescent peacock feathers.

Diandra had simply never encountered a being like the one standing in front of her now. His eyes fixed her with his stare and brought her back from her observations. She delightedly saw Altazar, yes, her beloved, looking at her from those solemn eyes with the slightest of friendly crinkles in the corners. She slowly smiled in full recognition and bowed with her head. A warm smile broke through the power of his countenance and he too bowed at her. Then Altazar stepped forward and outstretched his hands, palms downward, in the ancient Atlantean way of transmission of energies among initiates. She offered her hands to him, palms up—not touching his, and felt the glow of the sun entering her hands, traveling up her arms and throughout her body. She felt the toughness of the warrior that he was, felt his loneliness and then his yearning, felt his appraisal and acceptance of her. Then the sun warmed through her again.

Next he moved his hands below hers—palms up—and waited. Diandra realized the full implications of what he was offering. He was acknowledging her as his equal. As she moved her hands to the palms down position above his, this time it was Altazar who experienced her. He saw his strangeness to her and her fascination with it. He knew that she was fully aware of his need for her on all levels, that she brought into his life the Feminine Balance he had long sought. Seeing Diandra in the austere life of the Atlantean temples, he knew of her devotion, how she had taken her lessons and tasks seriously. He saw her work with the lesser initiates and how they held her in so much love and respect. Altazar also felt her loneliness, the deep yearning inside the heart of a highly evolved woman who has not yet found her mate, and who cannot settle for anyone less than her equal.

Taking her hands in his, he stared deeply into her eyes. Finally he let go her hands and said, "Come."

Thus did the meeting take place between Altazar and Diandra. Thus did they know of each other for the first time. And thus did their love burst into flower. (You may want to ask how I know of these things? Through the power of the crystals I was there and saw everything.)

CHAPTER THREE:
THE UNION

The sea breeze brought a fresh coolness—a welcome relief from the days of near-tropical heat. It was summer in Moragong, Altazar's capital city. Yes, it was the month of festivals and the nights were filled with the numerous gossamer sounds of music and singing mingled with the constant vibrations of bells and gongs. The air was fragrant with the myriad scents of exotic flowers in the fullness of blossoming. The many celebrations lasted throughout the long nights and it seemed as if the people rarely slept. Yet the populace didn't appear tired; they glided with a sure grace up and down the terraced hillsides tending the gardens and fields by day, always with a song and a smile. The festivals were held in honor of the abundance of the harvests, the plentiful supply of fish, the well-regulated weather. They offered the people an opportunity to show their respect to the Nature Spirits and to their enlightened ruler, Altazar, and strengthened their connection with the Sun, Moon and Stars. During these celebrations everyone participated—man, woman, and child. Each one shared of himself in song and dance and each one contributed offerings which regardless of how humble, were presented with utmost sincerity.

Altazar and Diandra were kept constantly occupied during this period, for their presences were required at each and every festival. It was considered a blessing for all, since the High King and Queen represented their direct link to the Gods and the Higher Energy Source. Altazar and Diandra traveled throughout this month visiting many of the more remote villages on the large island of Arnahem. They too, slept little, entering into that light-headed, floating, peaceful state of being that everyone was experiencing. This was the Month of Connection.

Altazar and Diandra now worked as one. Even when their duties caused them to be apart—the link, their unity of Purpose, was alive and they experienced no separation. They were in constant telepathic contact. It was as if part of Altazar resided within Diandra and part of her was within him. They had achieved a unity of souls rarely experienced before or since that distant Golden Age.

Altazar felt a completeness, a wholeness of manifestation that he had not known before. It was as if he and Diandra had each individually held parts of the same puzzle. They both brought to their union different strengths and weaknesses and areas of knowledge. Together they were in the process of putting together the entire picture. Indeed, he loved her tenderly and was deeply grateful that this particular woman had been assigned to be his partner. "I guess that the Great Source knows perfectly well what it is doing when it creates our lives' unique patterns and destinies," he thought. "I have been truly blessed by this woman. She is a strong confirmation for me of who I am."

One afternoon they were lounging comfortably in one of their palace's many gardens. This one contained several bubbling fountains. The water tumbled over the red and black volcanic rocks with which the island abounded, sending soft sprays of fine mists over the plant life, refreshing everything. The lush trees had cascading branches bent low with the weight of delicate fruits. A peacock lazily strutted back and forth opening his magnificent tail feathers for the benefit of several peahens. Diandra's favorite parrot perched nearby, lending its occasional comments to the scene.

Slowly stretching, Diandra removed herself from Altazar's encircling arms, then languidly walked to a nearby tree where she plucked a cluster of pink fruit, dipped it into the fountain, and returned to Altazar. Then as she fed him some of the fruit, she marveled at the fullness she felt. She had changed much since arriving here years ago. A new softness and gentleness had emerged. She felt a delicate glow surround her. This was caused by Altazar's presence in her life, that she well knew. His strong masculine protection had enabled her to open up many parts of her being that she had only faintly touched upon back in her former life in Atlantis. In her inner life, there were new developments as well. She was opening up to new energies, communicating with ever more distant universes. This, also, was the legacy of her union with this extraordinary man— without his balance and grounding of her energies, she would not venture into some of the realms which she now regularly frequented. She settled closer into his embrace, breathed deeply of his Divine Essence and smiled contentedly.

Altazar had been lost in thought for some time. Suddenly he broke their silence. "I am called upon to make a journey, but for some reason which I know not, it does not sit well in my heart. The Council of Tana wants me to go to the distant outpost island of Rapan-Nui to settle some dissident energies. I have undertaken similiar commissions many times before quite willingly, but something does not feel right to me about going this time," he explained.

Diandra stirred and put herself into her Higher Awareness. "When do they want you to go?" she inquired.

"Soon—within a few days, as soon as the Festival Cycle is complete," he answered.

"What would happen if you declined to go?" Diandra asked.

"That, I know not. I have always heeded their summons. In the hierarchial chain, I have no right to refuse. Yet, something troubles me about it."

Diandra looked into the matter. She took herself to the faraway island of Rapan-Nui. She saw the corruption that had been subtly insinuating itself into the life there. She saw as well that there would be no difficulty for Altazar to clear it up. So she turned her focus to Arnahem. Suddenly her sight froze and a beam of deep purple light entered her consciousness. This was symbolic of the Highest Authority. The voice of the Elder of the Brotherhood of the Seven came to her.

"Stop! You must not interfere with this. You are *not allowed* to use your gift of sight upon this matter. You are hereby commanded not to influence this process. Speak of it no further!" the voice intoned.

Diandra stiffened. Something of utmost importance

was about to happen and she was not allowed to look at it, much less use any of her powers to prevent it, if need be. But she was wise enough to respect the authority of the Seven.

Altazar looked at the stricken appearance of his beloved's face, and mistook it as her feeling of sadness at his impending departure. Taking her hand, he said, "Well, Diandra, I know that I must go on this journey, but please do not worry. I have done this work many times before and it will not be long before I return to you."

Tears ran down Diandra's grieving face. Pulling him closely to her, she murmured, "Oh, my noble Altazar, know that I will always love you. I will always remember you. I will always be with you in some form or another. Please, do not forget me. *More importantly, Altazar, please don't ever forget who you are!"*

"How could I ever forget you, my beautiful Altantean woman, you who have created the fullness in my heart," replied he while thinking, "What does she mean by saying, 'don't ever forget who I am?' Besides, I shall not be gone for long." Then extending his arm to her, he said, "Come, let us prepare ourselves for tonight's festival."

******

Thus it came to be that Altazar and Diandra were to be parted for many an age. (Oh, Altazar, if you could have but heeded Diandra's admonition to you. Then, perhaps, your destiny would have been kinder.)

But thus it was as I heard it with my very own ears in that lovely garden on that distant day.

CHAPTER FOUR:
THE MOTHER EGG

It was night on the main Lemurian land mass. A black night where billowing dark clouds raced across the sliver of amber moon. The Call had gone out—the Call of Utmost Urgency. The High Priests came quickly, tightly clutching their ceremonial robes against the wildly blowing wind. They entered the Temple of the Dawn one by one, knowing the seriousness of the Call that had summoned them here at this late hour.

The Council of Tana assembled in the high tower room, seating themselves in their accustomed chairs around the massive circular table carved from a single black volcanic stone, highly polished into a glowing brilliance. Yes, nearly all were present. Thirteen seats were occupied, that left three empty.

A low gong filled the tower with its vibrations. Og-Mora waited until the sound completely faded away. Yes, Og-Mora was still the Elder even though he had served in this capacity for thousands of years and his powers were finally beginning to weaken. Og-Mora's hair was snowy-white, his face a crevasse of deep wrinkles, his once proud carriage now stooped; yet, his eyes though sunken, contained a penetrating fiery glow. There was not a doubt that he still maintained much of his power and authority. His will somehow kept his aged form alive. Og-Mora was driven to see it through to the end. And tonight he was going to announce to the Council that the end was imminent; that is, if there was enough time remaining to explain it all before the impending catastrophe. It could not be transmuted nor prevented, of that he was certain. He had tried everything.

By now the others must have surely noticed that three of them were missing. Altazar's absence was easily explained. They all knew that he had been sent to Rapan-Nui on some Council business. Og-Mora smiled inwardly at the memory of Altazar. He had always been his favorite, the one whom he had been waiting for to succeed him. How ironic, now that Altazar was fully prepared, it was all to come to an end. That Atlantean woman whom he had been mated with had certainly hastened his growth. Yes, Altazar was his secret experiment, the first to be sent away covertly to the Atlantean temples, the first to marry someone from that other civilization so different from their own. He would have been a fine ruler for all of Lemuria—his own thriving island of Arnahem was proof of that. Well, at least he had managed to spare Altazar from the coming destruction. It had been his secret plan to remove Altazar from danger. Therefore the finest fruit of the Lemurian civilization would remain alive on this earth to carry on. Og-Mora regretted that he could not save the Atlantean woman as well, but sending her off with her husband would have awakened suspicion that something was amiss. Oh well, knowing her people, she would probably manage to return to Atlantis with little suffering.

Og-Mora now directed his thoughts to the other two men who were missing tonight. First there was that innocent fool Seplik. He saw Seplik's broad savage face with its flaring nostrils. Seplik was from one of the remote outer islands, the first from there to attend the Council. Wilder people habitated there who had missed many of the refinements learned on the mainland. Naive Seplik who would hereafter be known as *"The One Who Put Out The Heart Of the Fire."* Save who would survive to have any memories?

Og-Mora sat lost in his thoughts and the Council waited patiently and tuned into them. A pang of sadness brought him to the remembrance of the third one absent tonight. Bog-Lor, yes, it was he. He was the seed of this corruption, the one among them with the fatal flaw. Bog-Lor, the second only to himself. The one who had longed for hundreds of years to usurp him. Poor Bog-Lor who loved power so intensely. He craved it and manipulated it until finally it had taken him over and devoured him. His wisdom had been slowly clouded and his judgement distorted as he developed his mad magic in private. Longing not only to control Lemuria, Bog-Lor also secretly planned to make war upon and conquer Atlantis which he detested. He had long been jealous of the superior Atlantean technology and harbored bitter memories of being rebuffed by their Priests/Scientists, the Makers, when they had refused to share their precious secrets with him.

Thus Bog-Lor had pondered and plotted. He could not match Og-Mora's immoveable will power. He could not unseat him by ordinary means. So he needed a Plan. Bog-

Lor was one of the few who knew of the existence of the Mother Egg which held all life in balance on Lemuria. He also knew that the Mother Egg was hidden somewhere within the heart of the giant volcano, Karak-oa, the sacred mountain of Lemuria. Hence Bog-Lor devised a grand scheme of blackmail, threatening the very existence of Lemuria itself. There was simply no other way to defeat Og-Mora. That ancient, wily one would never yield his authority unless their entire survival was at stake.

So Bog-Lor isolated himself in his dwelling for many months, homing in on the energies of the Mother Egg until finally he contacted it. Then in his silence he began to see it, faintly at first as if in a haze—a reddish glow through the mists of time. He increased his concentration upon it until slowly it emerged into his vision. At last, after months of one-pointed contact, the picture was clearly focused. The Mother Egg was a bright ruby crimson egg-shaped crystal around fourteen inches in length. Inside it were fissures causing refractions which sent out intense beams of light. Soon he could pin-point its resting place within a small cave deep in the crater of Karak-oa.

Bog-Lor now needed a confirmation of his information in order to set his plot against Og-Mora into motion. Hence he brought Seplik into the plan. Seplik was simple, but he was also ambitious. He practically worshipped Bog-Lor who had impressed him with displays of his magic. Seplik constantly begged to become his apprentice so that, he too, could influence people. So Seplik entered the scenario. *(Has there ever been a time when power did not corrupt?)* Seplik was told that he was finally to be accepted by Bog-Lor as his disciple. First, however, he had to undergo a test of his commitment. For this initiation he was to go down deep inside the crater of Karak-oa, enter a certain cave and look upon a red glowing stone. Then he had merely to return to Bog-Lor who would be waiting for him on the volcano's edge.

Seplik readily agreed to undergo this task and henceforth set off with great excitement. The volcano was belching smoke and steam filled the air, burning his skin and singeing his nostrils each time that he breathed. *(Yes, it has been noted that Seplik was simple, but he was also strong and courageous, thus he carried on.)*

Finally, after many severe struggles, Seplik arrived at the heart of the crater. Here the molten lava bubbled continuously. The air was full of burning cinders whose sparks would often alight on Seplik, setting afire his clothes and hair. Shouting out in pain, he beat out the fires and continued on. This Seplik was from such tough stock that he never once considered fleeing from his ordeal.

Suddenly Seplik spied the entrance to the cave. It was located exactly as it had been described to him. With great excitement and a growing sense of relief, he entered its forbidden doorway. Instantly Seplik was surrounded by the most pervading darkness he had ever experienced. Slowly he could make out a brilliant red light emanating from the back of the cave. Cautiously, he stepped closer and closer towards it. Then he saw it fully. It was resting in a black stone basin. Red beams of light streamed forth from it in multiple directions. The Mother Egg was an oval-shaped crystal in whose depths could be seen the Life Blood itself.

Seplik was transfixed. He could not move or breathe. He just stood and watched the pulsations of the life force within that Egg. The vibrations of a heart-beat coursed through his body, sending a roar through his senses. He began getting very nervous—maybe it was the heat or maybe it was the lack of air. The sound was getting louder and louder until it was screaming throughout his being. Seplik ran to the egg-shaped crystal—ran to touch it or pick it up or something—this we never knew. But when his fingers touched it, Seplik was shocked to discover that it was soft, very soft, gelatinous—and one of his rough fingers pierced the outer membrane of the Mother Egg, causing a red transparent liquid, a terribly glowing liquid, to slowly ooze out of the puncture.

Seplik screamed in absolute terror. His scream was drowned out by a terrifying rumble of pain, a thunderous cry from the heart of the volcano itself. Seplik, his eyes frozen in fear, ran from the cave and threw himelf into the nearest pool of bubbling molten lava and disappeared— sinking without a trace.

At the same time, old Bog-Lor was sitting on the rim of the volcano deep in meditation, concentrating on the Mother Egg. Then he saw it. He saw the desecration. He saw their life blood flow away. He saw it slowly dripping out of that wondrous crystal and in that instant he knew. In that very moment of seeing, his appearance aged thousands of years. Then, when there was little flesh left on that haggard skeleton of a body, Bog-Lor pulled himself weakly to the crater's edge and plummeted down into the raging fires below.

** ** ** ** **

Thus it ended for Seplik and Bog-Lor. You might want to ask me what became of them. After such a destructive act, would they ever be allowed to return to the Earth?

Well, just to set your curiosity to rest, I will tell you—for I have watched it unfold since the Beginning. I will reveal everything so that I may finally forget.

Bog-Lor saw the profound error of his ways at the moment of desecration and has long since repented. He is here among us now. Ask me not—who is he?—where is he? That you must recognize yourself.

As for poor Seplik, please remember that although he was the instrument of a terrible crime, he had acted from innocence and ignorance. He has returned here many times, finally developing the wisdom that he has long sought. Today Seplik is one of our most devoted servants.

CHAPTER FIVE:
THE DREAM

That very night Og-Mora slept fitfully; his unconscious was not at peace. Finally lapsing into a dream state, he saw himself taken back to the time of the Beginning. He witnessed the creation of Lemuria, the Motherland.

A beautiful young woman appeared. She walked through the air towards him. She was holding some sort of precious bundle wrapped in cloth. At first Og-Mora thought that it might be a baby, but it was not. She slowly approached a stone cairn that had a smooth round basin carved out of the top of it. A bed of black sand rested inside the basin. The woman paused in front of the basin and lifted her bundle skyward, offering it to the Sun. She uttered some prayers, the words of which were so ancient, that even Og-Mora—as old as he was—could not make out their meaning. *(I shall tell you that she spoke in the seed tongue of this planet, which has ever been known to only a few.)*

Then she set her bundle down very carefully upon the

center of the basin. As she unwrapped the cloth, tears began streaming down her cheeks. She cried out with the anguish of all mothers giving birth for the first time. And then, there it was, unwrapped, lying silently in that dark basin. Og-Mora saw the Mother Egg! Time stood still or simply did not exist. The Sun shone steadily overhead. The woman cried ever more tears and raised her arms sunward as she intoned her ancient prayers over and over. The Sun moved directly above her and reached the full brilliance of its zenith. Then it sent a blindingly bright shaft of Light downwards-earthwards-ever nearer, until it reached the Silent Egg resting in the basin. A crack of thunder broke the stillness at the moment of penetration. The woman dropped her arms limply to her sides and cried no more. The Egg, that wondrous Egg, began to glow red, began to radiate vitality. Og-Mora could see it all so clearly. How the entrance of the Sun had caused the fissures within the Mother Egg's crystalline dimensions, sending out ruby red refractions of Light.

Og-Mora watched entranced as the young woman soon caused a small opening to appear in the base of the cairn. After she crawled into it, the opening sealed itself behind her.

The sky was rapidly turning darker and filling with debris. Rocks, ashes and smoke choked the pungent air. Then Og-Mora could see nothing but blackness for awhile. When the atmosphere finally cleared, there in the place of the stone cairn stood Lemuria's ancestral mountain, the formidable volcano, Karak-oa.

Og-Mora awoke shaking and drenched with sweat. He was profoundly affected by what he had just witnessed. Getting up, he splashed some cold water on his face. He tried to pray. He paced to and fro with troubled stride. Finally he managed to calm himself down. Then he heard a voice deep within him saying that he must return to sleep—that there was more to learn.

Og-Mora lay down and immediately fell into another deep sleep. This time he found himself inside a small cave deep within the heart of the volcano itself. It took him several moments before he could adjust his eyes enough in order to see a large stone roll away from what appeared to be that same cairn from long ago. Through the opening emerged the figure of a tiny, unspeakably ancient woman. Og-Mora was truly shocked at the sight of her. Although he, himself, had lived for several thousands of years, never before had he seen anyone *this* old. There seemed to be no bones, no substance to her, and yet—there she was standing before him. Her eyes were filled with a combination of deep sorrow and wisdom. They stared at him intensely. Og-Mora felt the heavy weight of the knowledge that she held. Finally, she spoke thus:

"Og-Mora," she whispered faintly. "I am Ma-Ah. I am the Mother of All Things. I was placed here at the Beginning. I begat the Mother Egg which begat the Motherland which begat all things which live upon it and have ever existed here." Tears streamed down her wrinkled face as she spoke. "Og-Mora, I am here to tell you that the time for Lemuria is running out. Our Mother Egg has been pierced and its Life Force is dripping away."

Og-Mora then saw the events which had taken place within the volcano that very day. He perceived the desperate scheming of Bog-Lor and saw the demise of him and Seplik. Finally he was allowed to view the Mother Egg itself. With a shudder he observed the stream of luminous red liquid that was slowly draining out of it.

"No," he said. "No!" He shook his head wildly in disbelief. "There must be some way to prevent this!"

"No, Wise One, there is not." Ma-Ah spoke in a tone of compassionate finality.

"How much time is left for us then?" Og-Mora incredulously asked.

"Not more than eight days at the most. It is finished. It has been decreed that Lemuria shall be no more. Accept this, for it is the truth." Ma-Ah's eyes filled with a look of fatigue and hopelessness. Suddenly she appeared even more frail and forlorn—standing so small and alone in the darkness. "Please, go warn your people. Some of them may be able to escape. Og-Mora, I say unto you that Lemuria is doomed. Go in peace and fulfill your final duty."

And thus she grew fainter and fainter until the merest wisp of shadow remained—then there was nothing save a plaintive memory. Og-Mora was left alone. Carrying the burden of his heavy responsibilites, he had never been more alone.

And thus did the End draw near for the Motherland.

CHAPTER SIX:
THE CRYSTAL CAVE

"**N**o!" The shout broke the silence of Og-Mora's chamber. The scream, his own terrible scream, had awakened him. Og-Mora sat up in bed, pale and trembling. An icy cold fear gripped his insides. Yes, he had no doubts. He didn't need any proof. He was absolutely certain that his dreams had held the truth.

"What to do? What to do?" he pondered endlessly. "I must devise a plan; there must be some way to prevent this. Whom dare I tell about this? No one, because the tidings will leak out and there will be frightening, horrifying panic." He thought of Altazar, his favorite, with a pang of regret. "I will save one of us, if I cannot save all of us and it shall be he." Hence he conceived the scheme to send Altazar to Rapan-Nui and put it into effect the first thing that very morning.

Then Og-Mora went alone to that most hidden place— the secret tower at the Temple of the Dawn. Slowly he climbed the ancient spiraling stairway and unlocked the door to the tower room, key trembling in his gnarled old hand.

Inside all was in darkness until he pulled the coverings off the opening to the sky. A burst of bright light flashed off the huge crystal in the center of the room. This crystal was a secret that he had shared with no one. It had been given to Lemuria long ago by the first Alta from Atlantis. It was to be used only in matters of utmost gravity, for it contained the power to communicate directly with the Nine via the magnetic grid. Well, now its time had come.

Og-Mora pulled himself erect by tightening the invisible golden cord which extended out of the top of his head. He arose into his Higher Awareness. He placed his hands over the crystal—not touching it physically—just letting their energy fields merge. He stroked the air around it. Og-Mora felt the power of the crystal activate as the air on his hands turned from cold to warm to hot. Then he uttered the Sound. The Sound that had been passed on to him, but only whispered once. The Sound that he had never before needed to utter. Staring into the crystal, he focused all his being into it. Then he stepped inside of it.

Og-Mora found himself inside a cavern. The cave was lined with transparent crystals, each emitting soft white light. Prisms danced back and forth from crystal to crystal. On the floor was a large eight-pointed star outlined in gold and lapis lazuli. Suspended or rather hovering, in the center of the star was a large globe of clear quartz filled with spiraling wisps of starry clouds. It floated about four feet above the ground.

Walking towards it, Og-Mora raised his hands in the ancient form of greeting. When he was nearly a foot away he stopped and felt the energy pouring into the palms of his hands. In an instant he felt the presence of others. Glancing around him, he observed nine figures clad in white robes. Eight stood at the points of the star. He noticed that they wore silver sashes tied with nine knots around their waists. Their faces could not be clearly seen, nor could Og-Mora perceive whether they were of male or female gender. The Ninth One stood opposite him on the other side of the quartz globe. This figure had its hands raised—palms towards him. Og-Mora noticed with some surprise that these hands had only four fingers each!

"Ah," he thought, "so the legend about the four-fingered ones is true," *(Alas, the hermit cannot divulge that legend to you at this point in the story, although some of you may already have that remembrance.)*

Og-Mora also observed that the being in front of him was wearing the slenderest of pure golden sashes hung low with eleven knots!

The old one from Lemuria stood quietly, his hands still raised towards the globe. His plea poured out through his thoughts. "The destruction of our Mother-land is near. Our Mother Egg has been fatally wounded. We have little time remaining. Can you not save us!" His emotions poured forth freely until finally there was silence once again. Og-Mora felt spent, but at peace. A sense of Oneness pervaded the cavern, a sense of timelessness, of unity.

A message was returned to him through his higher awareness. "The circle spirals itself back to the place of the Beginning. The cycle completes itself in perfection of its Purpose. Every Beginning containeth the seeds of its Completion. Everything that manifests itself into this world will also, one day, depart this world. When separation exists from the Oneness, there will always be a return to that Oneness. Now Lemuria is called to its dissolution. Its Higher Purpose has been served. Nothing can be done to further prolong its life span, for that goeth against the Law. Know well, Og-Mora, that the Motherland's destiny has been fulfilled. Go and see this cycle through."

Og-Mora was silent. His understanding was now complete. Bowing his head to them in gratitude, he closed his eyes. When he slowly reopened them he found himself back in the tower room. The giant crystal had disappeared. It had been apported back to the source from whence it had come.

Ah, poor Og-Mora, he knew, he understood, yet a profound feeling of sadness was within him. That old man carefully closed the opening to the sky and gently locked the door, knowing that he would never again return to the tower.

Arriving downstairs, he realized that it was now evening. Somehow seven days had passed by. Hence he called together the Council of Tana for its final emergency session.

CHAPTER SEVEN:
THE ASCENSION

As Og-Mora stood before the Council of Tana, he finished his reminiscenses and let his eyes—those ancient eyes which had seen so much—circle around the table. He looked deeply into the eyes of each of those present. Here and there tears glistened in the gazes which steadfastly met his.

"So, some of them knew already, did they? Well, all they had to do was to tune into my thoughts. The whole story is recorded there," Og-Mora mused.

"I call the Council of Tana to order," he announced with his greatest authority. "This shall be our final gathering. I have summoned you here to inform you that the hour of Lemuria's completion is at hand." He told them the stories of his two dreams. The Council sat ever so silently with a solemn respect for the overwhelming knowledge that they were receiving.

"Let us prepare to return to our places of origin in the far universes. Now we shall stand and hold each other's hands and experience the Oneness."

They stood and clasped hands. Some had tears running down their faces; others held expressions of raw courage. A few had to conquer the terrible fear inside that made them want to run outside shouting in panic. Yet there they stood and they stood as One. They felt their beings being pulled up by the golden cords. They were pulled up and up until their physical bodies became so light that they lifted off the ground. Still they stood— in the air now— holding hands—being One.

As they arose ever higher a great crackling roar of thunder exploded. The top of the temple blew off in the wake of numerous explosions. As they ascended, they saw the fires, the smoke, the newly created volcanoes gushing out streams of fiery red lava. They saw the cracks in the earth; they heard the horrifying screams of the people, the confusion of the animals. A chaos of destruction spewed its rage in all directions until, at last . . . . all was quiet.

Then Lemuria, the Motherland, rent into tiny fragments, gasped her final delicate sigh and slipped gently beneath the waves of the waiting ocean.

****

Thus came the End of the vast continent of Lemuria. I watched it all from my vantage point high above. Never have I wanted to relive a moment as terrible as that. But I have seen it, and even worse, repeat itself many times throughout the long course of the history of planet Earth. Can you not understand then my profound weariness?

CHAPTER EIGHT:
THE ISLAND

Far away, thousands of miles away, on the remote island of Rapan-Nui, it was a quiet summer's evening. Altazar rested in his thatched roof stone dwelling. Standing in the doorway he watched the sun descend over the sea's endless horizon, sending shimmers of reds and oranges over the undulating water. Monolithic stone figures stood watch over the island silhouetted against the brilliant sunset.

Rapan-Nui was a remote Lemurian outpost; nevertheless, it functioned as a major ceremonial center. A special caste of the priesthood lived and worked here in privacy, a secret that was kept from most of the Lemurian population. Their temples were discreet. Most of their rituals were performed outside in front of the stone guardians. *(Always when there is an outer place of power, there will be the corresponding inward place of power as well. And usually, if one must assign rankings of importance to such places, I always look to the hidden ones. For while the outward ones are the seats of politics and open wielding of authority, those hidden ones are thus freed to work on the pure level of spirit and can affect a profound influence on matters thousands of miles away, or indeed, far across the planet. Such a place was Rapan-Nui.)*

The priesthood here worked on the healing arts, utilizing highly developed skills of healing with the essences of flowers and plants. These were used in a preventative manner, concentrating more on correcting imbalances before they developed into diseases. This work was also known and practiced throughout Lemuria.

Their work also concerned alignments with certain star energies. Remember that Rapan-Nui was unique in its extreme isolation. The vastness of the heavens was more familiar to them than was the rest of the world. Hence they maintained strong connections with other extraterrestrial dimensions. The stone giants were conductors for this usage as well as protectors from negative energy patterns. They created a force-field of concentrated energy within the island which could then be used somewhat like a mirror to the heavens above. *(The real name of Rapan-Nui can no longer be spoken. It contains strong magic describing its true purpose which I am not permitted to disclose at this time. I will mention to you only that Rapan-Nui was also known as "The Eye Turned Towards The Sky." Perhaps you can discover its secrets on your own.)*

Altazar had been sent here to rechannel some corruption that had seeped into the temple hierarchy. His work had not been difficult. He had the clarity of vision—thanks in part to his secret Atlantean training to discern the untrue ones simply by looking into each ones' eyes. Then it was merely a matter of four days extensive reprogramming of the tainted ones' energies. To accomplish this he gave them certain combinations of the flower essences, prescribed by their own priests, in conjunction with administering treatment with certain crystals, *(another skill which he had refined in Atlantis).* The entire process had the effect of cleaning out the imbalances, through the flowers, and activating the energy centers which were too weak as well as neutralizing those that were too strong, through the use of crystals.

Tonight he had completed the four days of treatments and the healed ones had been released to return to their daily lives. They were cured and Altazar felt confident that they would present no further problems.

So this was to be his last night on the island. In the morning he would begin his return to Arnahem. He wished that Diandra had accompanied him on this journey. Yes, she would have found this secret outpost fascinating. But he had not been permitted to reveal to her the real function of this island. Of course, with her advanced sense of telepathy, she probably already knew all about it. She was an amazing woman indeed, so complex and strongspirited.

Altazar sat lost in his thoughts. The sun drifted below the ocean and all was in darkness. A peaceful night enveloped this magical isle so protected, so remote. Finally, Altazar laid his body down on his sleeping mat but could not sleep. A restless sense of anticipation kept him awake. He lay in the darkness and listened to the waves breaking upon the rocks below, feeling suddenly weary and old. He longed to be on his own island close to his beloved. Soon he felt Diandra's presence stir within him. She smiled at him and beckoned him closer. Altazar returned her smile and felt his heart fill up with radiating waves of love as if a fountain had been turned on inside of him.

Then it happened. A massive explosion followed by a series of terrible sounds coming from far, far away. Diandra's face changed from a smile to shock, then to extreme pain. Her image suddenly disappeared. Altazar jumped up and raced outside. Rapan-Nui itself was shaking with slight convulsive shocks and small pieces of it were breaking off and being swallowed by the ocean. The sky was a terrifying dark flaming red on the horizon. It was as if the sea and the heavens themselves were on fire. The sight of it filled him with horror. It contained the unmistakeable aura of destruction and death.

Altazar composed himself by using his warrior's skills. He tried to tune in once again with Diandra, but received no response. So he concentrated on Arnahem, but all he could see was a black, menacing, raging ocean. Moving his focus to the Temple of the Dawn, he called to Og-Mora himself. He had always been able to communicate with Og-Mora regardless of distance. He saw the Temple of the Dawn in ruins surrounded by blazing volcanic infernos.

"Og-Mora, what is happening?" he cried. But Og-Mora would not, could not appear to him. "Where are they? What has happened to Arnahem, to Lemuria, to my wife?" he raged.

Then he knew. Somewhere deep inside of him Altazar knew. It was finished. Lemuria had been destroyed. He knew not why nor how. But he knew that it was gone. His people, his island, his woman, his homeland, had all disappeared. Then in that horrible moment of knowing, a light was extinguished inside of him.

Altazar sank to his knees and wept.

CHAPTER NINE:
THE SURVIVOR

The sun arose over Rapan-Nui. Another dawn, another new day, but the world would never be the same. Lemuria had vanished save for a few small volcanic islands and atolls scattered here and there like stepping stones across the newly vast expanse of the Pacific Ocean.

Sea birds careened gracefully through the air, dove into the waves below and emerged with their prey. An air of normalcy prevailed—that is if you knew not the terrible truth. Small groups of the priesthood were already wandering around the island surveying the damage. Small chunks of Rapan-Nui had been submerged. Here and there a road would lead straight into the ocean and disappear. A few of the giant stone figures had toppled over, but basically, the island had survived and remained intact.

Altazar sat alone outside his hut. He had not moved all night. His eyes were fixed into an empty stare gazing hollowly out to sea in the direction of Lemuria. He had no thoughts, no emotions—just a bleak sense of overwhelming despair. He had already given full rein to his feelings during the endless night that had just passed. He had felt that he had let his people down by not being with them. Why did he have to survive and not them? Had Og-Mora known of this destruction in advance and sent him here in order to spare him? Knowing of Og-Mora's extreme fondness for him, that was entirely possible.

Altazar had not been able to endure the memory of Diandra's expression when that terrible thing had happened. She had definitely not been expecting it, that was certain. Why had her people on Atlantis not protected her? Why hadn't her psychic abilities warned her of the impending disaster? She had suffered incredible pain at the end; he had seen that too. Why had he not been there with her?

Now he was stranded on Rapan-Nui with no homeland to return to. He felt as if his life was over, as if he had failed his people and those whom he loved best. Altazar experienced guilt for the first time. It was that special guilt which survivors feel when they ask themselves why they were chosen to be spared and the others were not.

Feeling a tap on his shoulder, Altazar glanced up to see Solana, a young priest of Rapan-Nui who had aided him in his work here, take a seat beside him. Solana was tall and lithe with long dark hair and a handsome, almost androgynous face. His ear lobes had been pierced and extended with a large plug of white shell in the island style which had caused the Lemurians to refer to the inhabitants of Rapan-Nui as "The Long Earred Ones." Solana had been birthed here, had spent his entire life in the priesthood and had extremely clean energy. His large, unusual green eyes fixed Altazar with a look of penetrating clarity and compassion. Altazar suddenly realized how shattered he had become in contrast to the young priest who radiated health and wholeness.

Solana handed him a beaker of amber liquid. "Drink it, my friend," he quietly urged.

"Flower essences?" inquired Altazar hoarsely.

"Yes, they will help to heal the hole in your heart and give you strength."

Altazar drank the liquid dutifully, not caring if he was healed or strong.

Standing up, Solana said, "Come, my people want to talk with you," while motioning to the temple hidden within a nearby hill. He held out his hand to the exhausted Altazar. Together they walked to the temple, striding silently side by side. Altazar could feel warm healing energies emanating from the priest towards him. As they entered the portals of the temple, Altazar whispered his gratitude to Solana.

Passing through the entrance they proceeded down a long tunnel deep into the center of the hill. Finally the tunnel opened up into a large rectangular room. Several members of the priesthood were awaiting them, clad in simple sarong-type garments of various shades of green. Lighter skinned than most Lemurians, some of them had reddish hair and beards which was most unusual. *(It has been said that these ones were placed on this planet from a different energy source.)*

Altazar tried to remember who he was and act accordingly. But inside of him was that new feeling of hollowness and despair. He attempted to remember the proper forms of greeting and conduct. However, he could not bring his being into alignment; something was missing inside. His entire life had changed, that was the problem, he reminded himself while trying to pay attention to what was going on.

The priests were watching him intently, assessing the damage, trying to formulate a cure. Draughts of varying colored liquids were handed to him to drink and Altazar downed them numbly.

He was asked if he could use his crystals on himself. *(Altazar was the only one present with the full knowledge.)* Shaking his head in denial, he was denying not only the crystals, but that he even wanted to live. *(Note you here, that this was when denial entered his life.)*

Finally one of the priests spoke, "As you well know, the Motherland is no more. Someone has fatally damaged the Mother Egg. We are hereby sending you to Atlantis where you can obtain the full healing that you require. When Lemuria was ripped out from the magnetic grid, it tore a hole in your auric shield as well. Only the crystal therapy of restructurization can heal you completely. It will be a long, arduous journey. We no longer have the means here to teleport you. All of that was destroyed with the submerging of the main land mass. For teleportation we required the use of their generator crystal as an energy booster. So, you must travel by sea and overland through many strange and unknown lands, but nevertheless, Altazar, you must go."

Altazar nodded in mute understanding, feeling that he must surely be dreaming.

"Solana has offered to go with you for your added protection. He will be carrying messages for help from us to the Brotherhood of the Seven in Atlantis. We can spare no one else to go with you. Our future is now uncertain and we have much work to do here. Tonight we ask you to remain in the temple with us. We will attempt all the healing for you that is within our power. You will be departing Rapan-Nui in the morning by boat and sailing first to the south and then to the east. It will be difficult and lengthy due to the strong westward currents in this part of the ocean. The provisions are presently being readied for your journey. We shall tell you that no one has ever before attempted the voyage from Rapan-Nui to Atlantis, but it must be done. You must do this for all of us and for the memory of your people."

Altazar tried to listen, tried to pay attention to the words which were coming towards him from so far away, echoing blankly throughout his internal emptiness. All the while Solana observed the High King carefully with his finely attuned intelligence, knowing fully that the weight of this man and the success of this mission rested upon his slender shoulders. Somehow, he vowed, he would manage to carry it to completion.

**   **   **   **

Thus Altazar and Solana did prepare to depart the last vestige of the great Lemurian Empire to journey far into the Unknown. They knew not that they would never return to their ancient homeland. Can you stretch your awareness to see that I was there and saw it all?

CHAPTER TEN:
THE VOYAGE

It was morning. A small group of people carefully descended the edge of a steep, rocky cliff. Little remained of Orongo's tiny sheltered lagoon, most of it had now disappeared into the ocean. The boat waited patiently in the water, tied to a tree which had been felled by the tremors of a few nights ago. The vessel was built of totora reeds, from one of Rapan-Nui's marshy places hidden deep inside the crater of a volcano. It had a mast and reed sail and a small carved wooden cabin which was well-stocked for their long journey.

The priests that accompanied Altazar and Solana were chanting ancient songs of farewell in soft low voices. Another group stood clustered at the top of the cliff, singing melodiously while tossing exotic flowers onto the figures below.

Altazar and Solana bowed low to the priests. The Head Priest dipped two of his fingers into a bowl of a white pasty substance which he was holding. Then he traced delicate patterns with this onto the faces of our two travelers. This would serve to protect them during their voyage across the ocean.

An old man, called the Master of the Sea, gestured to Solana and spoke to him in low urgent tones. He handed him a weird web-like object made of reeds tied together into a maze of spirals. This was the map of the eastern ocean currents. They would be sailing a distance twice as far as that to Lemuria. Due to the unusually strong westward currents, they would first have to head south for quite a distance. Fortunately, Solana had used these maps before, since most of the island dwellers had been taught this knowledge since childhood.

Altazar stepped upon the boat and was surprised to discover how springy it felt. Light and fragile, it was quite unlike the sturdy Lemurian boats constructed from hollowed-out solid logs of wood.

Solana, his eyes alight with adventure, finally climbed onto the boat. It settled even lower into the water but somehow managed to float. In the morning sunlight Solana looked truly beautiful. Upon his face was painted a diagonal white line that had been filled in with delicate traceries. Young and radiant, his slender frame had such a grace to it that his very movements seemed like part of a ceremonial dance.

Nodding warmly to Altazar, he said, "So begins our great adventure!" Casting off the boat, Solana raised his hands high to the stone guardians of Rapan-Nui and began to sing his own song of farewell in the clearest of voices.

Taking the elaborately carved wooden tiller, Altazar smiled through his saddened eyes and even shared in a twinge of excitement for the adventure which lay before them. He felt better today, as well he might, for all night long the priests had sung over him, fed him essences of flowers, rubbed him down with fragrant plants—all the while chanting and praying.

"What an enchanted place, this Rapan-Nui," he mused. "No wonder that it was chosen to survive." Looking at Solana, he noted again his purity and clarity. "The people from this island are more similiar to the ancient Lemurians in many ways than we from the mainland are," he thought. "They, whether male or female, are difficult to tell apart, since each of them seem to contain both sexes within them. They are remnants of the days long ago when we used to be androgynous. They have experienced the division into the sexes as we have, but they seem to be complete and self-contained in a way that we have lost."

Completing his song, Solana picked up his reed map. Creeping cautiously to the front of the boat, he put his hand into the water, carefully sensing the shape of the currents and checking it against the map. Crouching inside the pointed prow, Solana began another song. *(It must be noted that these folk from Rapan-Nui were rather fond of singing, in fact they preferred song over talk.)* This one invoked the Spirits of the Vast Ocean, asking them for safe passage through their waters. When Solana had finished, Altazar laughed from the pure joy of the brilliant blue sky, the endless sparkling ocean, and of course, the joyous music itself.

Then the High King surprised himself by offering a song. This was in honor of the Water Dragons who live within the depths of every body of water throughout the world. His deep, resonating voice brought forth a song of such sad sweetness that it caused the very dragons themselves to cry. Their tears bubbled up to the surface throughout the vast ocean. Tears glistened in Solana's eyes as well as he quietly listened while straddling the prow, his bare legs dangling into the water. Next Solana chanted a happy, frolicking song about their friends, the whales and the dolphins.

And so the time passed tenderly and without crisis while they journeyed throughout the endless blueness, seemingly going to the end of the universe itself. The days sped by rapidly as did the nights. Nights when they would sit silently outside in the darkness enveloped in a shining cocoon of stars—always sailing onward and onward. As the weeks slipped by they became close friends, having shared much by now: the vast silence, the never-ending blue expanse of sea and sky, the canopy of stars at night. Opening up their souls to each other, they began sharing not only their experiences, their knowledge, their legends, but finally, many of their most private thoughts.

Weeks multiplied into months, the months added up and still they sailed. One day passed by much like the other with a certain timeless sameness. To Altazar, it was as if his past was dead, having faded away into his internal place of emptiness—disappearing slowly, steadily and imperceptibly. His life in Lemuria faded like a long-lost dream, ever more misty, ever more forgotten. He no longer felt like a High King of noble lineage—just a simple man on a small boat adrift on the vast ocean. The only reality that he knew for certain was being on this fragile bundle of reeds— sailing, sailing across the infinity of endless blue waves. There was incredible peace here for him. There was a soothing nothingness to it, and there was his remarkable new friend with whom to share the wonder of it all.

A vast expanse of time did indeed pass by, then at last, the day did come when they spied their first sea bird. In the days that followed they saw many others and realized with a mixture of sadness and excitement that soon they would be approaching land. After a few more days they saw a large land mass stretching across the horizon, covered with massive mountain ranges whose tallest peaks were capped by the sparkling whiteness of glistening snow. Solana stood in his place in the prow, arms outstretched in greeting, eyes glittering with anticipation, and burst forth once more into song. This one was a respectful greeting to the new land. Then after washing themselves, they changed into fresh garments and prepared to go ashore.

**** **** **** ****

Thus did our travelers put the shining, foaming sea behind them and enter upon an Unknown Land. Many wonders would await them there. Even I would encounter them there, though they knew not, as yet, of my existence. And Altazar, if ever you read these words, can you not see, can you not remember? This was when you began to forget yourself. I know that the cause was for your healing then. But now it is the time for you to awaken, remember and step forward to claim who you are!

CHAPTER ELEVEN:
THE APPROACH

The fragile reed boat had fulfilled its purpose and rested wearily upon the sandy beach. The shoreline resounded with the steady rhythmic crashing of wave upon wave. Sea birds circled constantly, filling the air with their haunting calls as they searched for silver glints of fish in the rippling waters below. In the distance loomed the shapes of enormous mountains standing as silent sentinels. Their jagged peaks cast mysterious shadows which revealed powerful and awesome glimpses into the guardian spirits of this strange land.

Our travelers finished preparing their supplies for the long trek ahead of them. There was little to take with them, for scant remained after their long time at sea. Then, bidding farewell to the now waterlogged boat, they began striding through the sand towards the beckoning majesty of the mountains. The coarse sand soon gave way to rocks, then the small rocks yielded to larger ones until they had climbed up and over what appeared to be one huge sheet of stone pitted with small holes in which water and marine life had collected themselves into miniature worlds. The peaks ahead gleamed with a coppery glint reflected from the sun.

They were now moving upon a rocky ledge on which a lone tree defiantly grew, pushing its life force up through the smallest of cracks. *(Curious, is it not, how sometimes the strongest of trees seem to grow in the most difficult of places while the trees who choose an easier environment often do not grow as hardy or as old.)* Near the tree the ledge widened out and there stood an upright stone slab carved with the symbol of the Sun above the crescent Moon. Both of them stopped to look at it with amazement.

"Altazar," Solana whispered reverently, "this is the symbol of the ancient Kingdom of AN."

Altazar looked up at the mountains which towered above them. "Yes, these must be the ANTES, the copper-covered mountains of which our legends speak." He gazed keenly at Solana's shining face which was filled with wonder. Then the understanding came to him. "Sol-an-a, you my friend, are one of those bound secretly in service to the ancient God AN, are you not?"

"Yes, Altazar, that is true. But to be here near the Kingdom of AN is beyond my wildest dreams. I knew not if AN ever existed on the physical plane."

Solana stood straight and tall and raised his arms high to the Sun chanting in an unknown tongue:

> *Homage to thee, O AN of ANTES*
> *Who doth stride across the sky*
> *Bringing balance of Sun and Moon,*
> *Melding the four directions*
> *Into One.*

Uniting all opposites,
Completing and Beginning
In a single breath.

O AN of ANTES,
Complete One,
As the hand is to the man,
As the ray is to the Sun,
I surrender my Self to you
In total loving service
That there shall be
Separation no more,
That all may know
Union into Oneness.

Meanwhile, holding a crystal to the sun, Altazar lit a small piece of copal and placed it respectfully at the base of the rock. He then began to explore their surroundings, finding a small stone path which disappeared behind some nearby cliffs. "We are well guided," thought he, "probably expected somewhere as well." *(How often have life's surprises been already known to others? —asketh the hermit.)*

Solana approached him quietly and gestured eagerly towards the pathway. "Come," Altazar smiled fondly, "let us discover your land of AN."

The rocky trail was narrow and steep but fairly secure, nevertheless, our travelers proceeded carefully. Soon they had climbed high up the side of the ridge and grew weary from the dizzy heights and change of altitude. The sun was now beginning to set over the ocean, a blinding sea of molten oranges, golds and reds stretching to the far horizon.

"Altazar, look at the Sun!" Solana exclaimed and began to sing in a voice filled with a plaintive nostalgia.

> *In the Dawn of Time*
> *The Sun was born of the Lake*
> *It arose—a fiery red glow*
> *And cast upon the waters*
> *A flaming path of streaming Light,*
> *Leaving a mirrored reflection*
> *Of itself in the Lake*
> *For men to follow.*
>
> *The Sun that we see*
> *In the sky above us*
> *Is but that reflection*
> *From the Waters of Time.*
> *It is our beacon to aspire to.*
>
> *But beyond our Sun, our Moon,*
> *Or this world itself*
> *Is the true Sun*
> *Glowing ever brighter,*
> *Waiting for our Return.*
>
> *Until that moment*
> *Follow the Golden Path*
> *Through the ripples*
> *It shall lead us Home.*

They stood silently for a time lost in contemplation. Then Altazar stirred himself and asked, "Think you that if we can find the Kingdom of AN that they will know of a faster way to get us to Atlantis?"

"If anyone on this planet other than our people or the Atlanteans themselves have this knowledge, they surely will," Solana answered confidently.

"Well then, let us proceed and try to find AN."

The path took a sharp turn around yet another rock ledge and they found themselves staring at the mouth of a hollowed-out cavern.

"A good stopping place for the night," Altazar observed. Solana nodded his agreement. And indeed, it must have been foreordained because they soon discovered in the back of the cave a stack of finely woven wool blankets and clay pots full of food and fresh water. Again Altazar had that strange premonition of being watched over. It did not seem to make him uneasy however, simply a little curious at the mysteries of this unknown land.

They slept deeply that night and awoke refreshed and eager to be on their way. The clay pots once again held fresh food and drink. Eating silently, they marvelled at the persistent presence of unseen forces. Then they proceeded upon their trek.

The path led ever upwards. A small stream joined it and the canyon walls on either side grew steep and narrow until they walked one behind the other. Altazar led the way carefully. He felt increasingly like a new person and less like the High King of Arnahem. Much had been dropping away after the sinking of all that he had known and loved and with the many miles that he had distanced himself from his memories. He felt more whole as long as he allowed himself to forget what had been and what was no longer.

The sound of water crashing over a cataract brought him back from his musings. A waterfall of about twenty feet in height was in front of them; the pounding water washed away the remainder of his broken memories. As the way ahead became impassable, it was necessary for them to climb up the wall of stone at the waterfall's edge in order to continue on. When they had reached the top, they noticed that the pathway once again followed the course of the stream, interrupting itself only to detour around other yet taller cascades of sparkling water. Finally they decided to stop for awhile and bathe in the cool clearness of the pools underneath one of the falls. Pulling off their garments, each got into adjoining rock basins. The water was very soothing as they submerged themselves and began to relax.

Altazar closed his eyes and felt the warmth of the sun on his face and the coolness of the water on his tired body. Letting go his thoughts he began drifting away, melting into the water. Suddenly the face of a woman appeared to him, her head wrapped in a silky white cloth so that only her eyes could be seen. They were incredible eyes, large and green, which shone with the Light of Far-Seeing Wisdom. They were eyes which saw through and beyond the veils of time and space. Looking deeply into his very soul as though scanning the Akashic Records of his being, she spoke thus to him:

"Altazar, my greetings to you! I bring you a message from the Place of Silence. I am the one known as the Hermit of the Crystal Mountain. You must find your way there. It is where true healing for you shall be found. However, know that the Crystal Mountain can only be entered in your crystal body of light. This you must develop. I shall ever be awaiting you there."

Looking at him with an aura which penetratingly radiated unconditional love, she continued. "When you arise from these waters you will find a magenta poncho waiting for each of you. Wear these with respect, for they shall be as shields for you. They will protect you when you least expect it and when your need is greatest. I am giving a conch shell trumpet to Solana. He will know when to sound its call. It shall serve him well. For you, I leave a special crystal. The knowledge encoded within its hidden spiral will guide you back into yourself at the appropriate time. It is a mirrored reflection of your purest Essence, a small shard of the star."

"My dearest brother, remember what I have told you and you shall have nothing to fear. Forget not the Crystal Mountain! No matter how long your journey, no matter what you have undergone, I shall not forget you and will await you there." Once again her eyes pierced deeply into him, fanning his very essence with love and tenderness. Then she slowly faded from sight.

Altazar remained quietly in the pool of water as her words repeated themselves throughout his consciousness. He sought to remember them all, to sear them into his memory, but they slowly slipped further and further into the unreachable depths of his unconscious despite his fervent efforts.

A call from Solana caused him to return to this reality. "Altazar, come here and see what I have found upon the grass!" He held aloft a conch shell of smoothest white. A delicately woven strap was attached at both ends so that it could be worn around the neck. "There is the mark of AN carved into this shell," he exulted. Altazar also saw the two ponchos of radiant magenta lying neatly folded on the grass.

"Solana, I must share with you the vision I had while

I was lying in the pool," Altazar quietly remarked. "A woman appeared in a vision to me; some sort of spirit woman. She was all wrapped up in a white cloth so that I could barely see her features, except for her eyes. I shall never forget those penetrating green eyes; they seemed to be from another world. They saw everything. This woman called herself the Hermit of the Crystal Mountain. Something about her was very familiar; I felt as if I recognized her although I am certain that I knew her not in Lemuria. She told me many wondrous things—that the conch shell is for you and the ponchos are for some sort of protection .... if only I could remember exactly what she told me. She did say something about how I must find my way to a Crystal Mountain to receive healing."

"Know you where that is?" Solana inquired with rising excitement.

"No, I have no idea . . . " replied Altazar—while the words in *a new land* flashed into his mind. Picking up his poncho, he discovered a shining quartz crystal of radiant clarity tucked within its folds. With a bemused smile, Altazar placed it inside the folds of his sarong.

Tossing the ponchos over their shoulders, they continued on their way once again until, at last, the sun began to set. Then they were pleased to discover a small stone hut set into the rock walls of the steep canyon. It was becoming increasingly difficult to determine if these walls were man-made or natural. The stonework was excellent but no mortar could be found—the rocks of varying sizes and shapes fitted perfectly together. Entering the hut they discovered the almost expected pile of colorful woolen blankets and the clay pots full of food and drink.

"This is indeed a strange and mysterious land," enthused Solana. He had not known such intense excitement before. He felt himself propelled towards some fantasic destiny which was impossible to deduce in advance. They could only surrender to it as it chose to reveal itself in the present.

Our two travelers ate heartily and prepared their beds, each placing a magenta poncho over himself. Even though their minds abounded with questioning thoughts, they soon sank deeply into sleep.

CHAPTER TWELVE:
THE CAPTURE

S ometime in deepest night—in those hours halfway between midnight and the dawning when strange and unknown things are free to enter—there came the otherworldly sounds of a flute. Its haunting melodies flickered from outside the hut to inside, from this side to that. Solana and Altazar both awoke but dared not move. Their keen eyes silently searched the darkness for the source of the sounds. Soon the voice of another flute joined in, then yet another, then many more. The music came from all directions at once and led their attentive ears from outside to inside, from down to up, leading their attention in a spiral dance upwards, then a reverse spiral down. Altazar and Solana were becoming increasingly disoriented and unnerved by the reverberating song. But each one of them continued to lie still and dared not speak a word to the other. The music cast a spell which took them deeper and deeper into a hypnotic trance.

As the music reached a crescendo, all the flutes repeated the same melody over and over at overlapping intervals. Suddenly all the instruments converged simultaneously into the same phrase at once. Then there was silence once again. Our travelers breathed not, moved not, but watched mutely from outside their frozen bodies. Then, lying there stunned in the darkness, they saw a strangely glowing spirit being clad in a loin cloth of palest blue, enter the hut—not through the door—but through one of the walls! Upon his long flowing black hair was a silver circlet supporting a tall headress of exotic plumes. This bizarre creature quickly threw a silver net over the sleeping forms of Altazar and Solana. Next he deftly scooped up the net which appeared to be weightless, even with the two travelers inside it, and walked through the wall of the hut. Outside, waiting impatiently with ears back, was a strange animal which looked like a combination of a deer and a camel with long shaggy white fur. The spirit being tossed the silvery net upon the animal's back and departed. Jumbled up in the net, Altazar and Solana fell victim to its moonbeam magic and went deeper into a strange and troubled sleep.

"Now, raise the net," a woman's voice commanded. The spirit being stepped forward and untangled the net from the silent bodies of Altazar and Solana. He threw the silver net high in the air whereupon it shrank and disappeared. Altazar and Solana slowly began to return to consciousness. Opening their eyes, they looked at each other with surprise. Then gazing around their surroundings, they were indeed astonished. They found themselves lying on the stone floor of a large rectangular temple. The temple was composed of gigantic stone blocks, many of which must have weighed several hundred tons each. There was an unseen lighting source in the room which cast an eery pale blue haze over everything.

In the center of each wall stood one of those strange spirit men with silvery headresses. These four were clad in pale yellow loincloths topped with ponchos made of brilliantly colored plumes. Altazar noted with interest that the one at the western side bore the design of a puma, that on the north—a condor, in the east where the rising sun streamed through an open doorway in the temple wall—he wore the fish, at the south—the symbol of man. Each of these unmoving guardians stared impassively straight ahead. It could not be said for certain whether they were alive or not, for although they appeared in human forms, there was an almost transparent quality to them.

Solana whispered to Altazar, "This is *not* the Kingdom of AN. Where are we? Know you anything of this place?"

A woman's soft low voice spoke to them from the opening behind them. "Welcome travelers to TI-WA-KU. I have been expecting you."

Turning around quickly, they saw the woman standing in the doorway assessing them with an air of confidence and power. She was handsome with a strong oval face. Her features contained not a visible flaw yet there was a subtle starkness about her. Maybe it was the pointed chin or the finely molded sharpness of her nose, the high delineated cheekbones or the almond shaped eyes—no, it was perfect, too perfect. She radiated raw cat-like strength and power—yes, too much power. Her raven colored hair was pulled up tightly to the top of her head, whereupon a braid began, coiling around and around, spiralling its way down her back.

Altazar moved his hand to his dagger as he heard a voice whisper inside him, "Beware!"

Then she smiled at him, filling him with her warmth and vast energy. "Altazar, you need not fear me," spoke she in a voice both reassuring and commanding. As she moved closer to him, her pale blue tunic swayed sinuously. He noticed that it was covered with subtle, interwoven symbols of puma/fish/condor/man. Her imposing body was large-boned and ample but somehow gave the appearance of slenderness.

The High King let go his caution and disregarding the warning I had just given him, arose and bowed low to the woman. "How know you my name?" he asked, mystified.

"Let us just state, that although we are not of this world, we are aware of it when it moves within our sphere," she replied in her unusual voice that rippled from nuance to nuance.

"May I ask you for your name since you seem to be familiar with mine?" Altazar inquired while basking in the bolt of energy that she had directed fully upon him.

"I call myself Mu'Ra. . . I call myself the Last. I call myself the Only since I am the only one who remains. The others have all returned—far, far away."

"What do you mean that you are the only one here? What about those guards against the walls?" Altazar gestured to the spirit/men in their feathered ponchos.

Mu'Ra raised her hands high, spreading open wide her fingers. Our travelers stared at her in profound shock, feeling penetrating shivers descend down their spines as they both noticed that she had only four fingers on each hand!

"I am the Last . . . The Final One. The others have gone," she repeated forcefully.

During all this time, Solana had been sitting quietly watching everything from his position on the floor. His presence seemed to have been momentarily forgotten, allowing him to observe it all intently with his Higher Awareness. He knew well that this was *not* AN—the energy patterns were far different from it. Here everything was imbued with a pale blue and yellow haze. He rolled the word, TI-WA-KU through his consciousness . . . feeling that somewhere, at some distant time perhaps, he had encountered it before. And what was the significance of the puma/fish/condor/man symbols? The woman Mu'Ra he did not trust, although Altazar obviously did. There was something in the warmth of her smile, in the eyes which glowed with sincerity, and the undulating magic of her voice, that gave him an uneasy sensation in his solar plexus and that warning hum in his third eye. Both were signs that he knew well to respect.

"Something is indeed strange here," he mused. "There is a heavy, hidden, dark secret that I must discover." And then when she had revealed her four-fingered hands, he had understood more. She was obviously not of this planet but from some other highly evolved galactic system. Solana was familiar with such alien visitors to earth. He had often been involved in ceremonies on Rapan-Nui which communicated to those Starry Beings who watch over us on this planet and to whom some of us are bound in brotherhoods of service and wisdom.

"But this woman is somehow treacherous. Why was she left here alone? What does she desire of us?"

Solana had never imagined that Starry Beings could have their energies tainted and distorted and fall from grace as indeed humans were prone to do.

"Strange, was it not, that just when we were approaching so near to AN," he was positive that the food and blankets had been provided by AN, not TI-WA-KU, "that we would find ourselves detoured here where the energy pattern is so different."

Solana wondered if they were prisoners and whether they would be permitted to leave whenever they wished. Altazar definitely did not regard himself as a captive. His eyes were enraptured as Mu'Ra's whispery voice glided around him.

". . . yes, for a long time we have been an important ceremonial center, but not for the world of men. We have, on occasion, permitted some earthly people to enter our portals, but after completing the full initiatory cycle, they rarely wish to return to whence they came. Hence we are unknown in the world and have remained secret for countless thousands of years."

"What have become of all the people who have trained here?" asked Altazar.

"When they are fully prepared they ascend to what I shall term the parallel dimensions."

"And what are they?" Altazar leaned forward in total absorption.

"Altazar, my dear friend, that can only be revealed after

you have been schooled in the mysteries which I alone hold." Her voice insinuated hidden secrets of distant universes, of bountiful treasures of forbidden knowledge. At this point in time, Solana chose to rise and make his presence known. He moved close to Altazar's side and tapped him firmly on the back in a special spot, causing him to return somewhat to his senses. Altazar straightened up and seemed to be surprised to see Solana—as if he had forgotten him entirely!

"Ah yes, Mu'Ra, may I present to you my good friend and traveling companion, Solana, priest from the island of Rapan-Nui."

Solana bowed his head slightly to Mu'Ra, careful not to allow any shade of expression or emotion to reveal his impressions of their situation. Mu'Ra shot him through with a shaft of terrible raw power, yet Solana moved not— standing lightly balanced on his center of clean, innocent clarity.

"Solana, if you be a friend of Altazar, then you are welcome here as well." Mu'Ra smiled at him sweetly and again Solana experienced a cold premonition of danger. "Both of you must be weary from your long travels so I shall dismiss you to your chambers." She gestured imperiously to the figure who had captured them to lead them out. Entering a courtyard, they noticed that the sunlight itself contained a pale blue haze to it, emanating a peculiar feeling of unnaturalness to everything.

"Beautiful here, isn't it?" remarked Altazar.

Solana gazed quietly at his friend, feeling an unfamiliar sense of sadness begin to choke his heart. He could say nothing yet, silently observing it all until he finally understood what was truly in play. But he knew with great clarity that he must somehow get Altazar to leave this place with him. And within the painful sense of grief that lay heavily inside his chest, Solana knew that it would not be an easy task.

*   **   ***   **   *

Thus did Altazar encounter the alien woman Mu'Ra. I did warn him, but he listened to me not. (Oh Altazar, how long must it be before you awaken?) Please remember that you were never forgotten. I came to you many times. I watched over you always. I marvelled at your great courage, for the vastness of what you had chosen to take on and transmute for all of us. If only you could see that for yourself.

CHAPTER THIRTEEN:
ATLANTIS

L et us leave Altazar and Solana for awhile. They are lost from time anyway. We shall trace our way far across the world to the mighty continent of Atlantis. And if you will permit me to use some of my magic on you, we shall also thread our way back in time—to those awful moments when Lemuria was at the brink of its destruction.

The Atlantean Priesthood had been aware in advance of Lemuria's prophesied end. The piercing of the Mother Egg had been witnessed and reported by one of their oracles. The Nine knew. They had searched on their own for a way to alter Lemuria's terrible fate even before Og-Mora had appeared before them. But the Motherland's destiny had already been sealed by the Higher Forces. The Brotherhood of the Seven had been duly informed by the High Priestess Alorah *(was she not one of the Nine?)*. The Elder of the Seven had likewise communicated this to the Alta himself. He, the highest Atlantean leader, wielder of temporal power, then alerted the secret society of priests/ scientists called the Makers.

The Makers worked in secret upon the hidden back part of the hill from which Diandra had departed Atlantis. They had vast underground laboratories connected by miles of labyrinthean tunnels wherein they were engaged in research of a most experimental nature. Some of this involved the use of sound and crystals, and had even included what is now known as nuclear energy at one point, although that had been discontinued due to the obvious danger involved. The Makers entered not into the everyday life of Atlantis, but lived within the hill in monastic confinement. Their lives were absolutely dedicated to their experiments and discoveries. Due to the powerful forces that they dealt with, holding the very seeds of creation and destruction in their hands, it was considered essential that their energies remain untainted by contact with worldly concerns.

Only one of them was allowed complete freedom of movement and that was the formidable Dr. Z. *(Dare we mention his name, even now?)* So vast was his knowledge, so awesome his personal power, that only he and the Alta himself, had absolute access to everything on Atlantis. Dr. Z. could communicate directly with the Nine, attend the most private councils of the Seven, and was the sole controller of the magnetic grid. Only he understood it totally, holding the golden key to the Master Grid. He was the power behind the throne, so to speak, who preferred to work behind the scenes, influencing all aspects of Atlantean life. Yes, Dr. Z. was a legend complete in himself— held in awe by all, in fear by many, and in love by few— mainly his beautiful and talented daughter Namuani.

This woman was famed throughout Atlantis for the healing music she created in the Temple of Sound, or ENORA. Namuani made this extraordinary music by moving her hands above a giant slab of man-made crystal, and once heard, the sounds were never forgotten. They contained the capability to align the chakras, to heal the etheric, astral and physical bodies, or to initiate into the Mysteries. If misused, this music had immense power to destroy—even thousands of leagues away. For this reason very few people were ever permitted to be initiated into the secrets of the creation of this form of music.

Namuani resided in the Temple of Sound with her two children, the boy called Anion and his younger sister Novasna. Her husband was the famed Master Vanel, the greatest musician in the entire history of Atlantis. Vanel had long ago given up performing in public in order to concentrate on the absolute essence of pure sound. Save for the Master Vanel, Namuani was the most accomplished of the handful of musicians in the Temple of Enora. Namuani's young daughter Novasna had been fathered by Vanel with whom she shared enduring love and mutual respect.

The eldest of her children, the sensitive Anion, was sired by one of the Makers named Davodd. Namuani had known him since childhood when he had not yet been chosen as a Maker nor moved to the hill. Davodd was a wild genius, darkly handsome, passionate and unpredictable. After they had separated as lovers they remained as friends and often Namuani and her children would visit him upon the hill outside the House of the Makers. Because Namuani's father was Dr. Z. and since no one dared to question his authority, she was given the secret password and magic gesture which opened the golden gate at the base of the hill.

Upon this day she and Davodd visited on that secret

hill. Nearby her children played quietly together, imagining themselves as small insects exploring the wild jungles of grass which they sat upon. The game had begun when Novasna had noticed a tiny insect crawling through the dense foliage of grass. She realized that to the insect the small blades of grass were as a jungle, while to her the same grass was simply like a carpet under her feet. Calling her big brother to her side with excitement, she patiently explained the wonder of how two very different worlds could exist only inches apart within the same dimension. Hence they decided to pretend that they, too, were small in order to investigate further that other world. *(If you really think about this, you shall understand the secrets of what are termed the simultaneous dimensions.)*

The afternoon was full with the freshness of spring as Namuani sat happily upon the grass, her long wavy hair loose and billowing in the soft breezes. She had large, velvety dark eyes on a long, slender frame which gave her a deer-like grace. Her person radiated quiet, self-contained inner peace with a strong, loving heart. Although born and brought up within the top caste of the Atlantean hierarchy, Namuani was unspoiled and dedicated to serving her people. She served with courage and compassion and was much beloved and rather well known throughout Atlantis.

Today she watched Davodd with quiet bemusement. He was obviously distraught and agitated. His black eyes brooded with a stormy genius that contained a slight hint of madness. Davodd loved Namuani dearly as his sole friend in Atlantis, although they no longer shared feelings as man and woman.

"Nami," (He called her by her childhood nickname.) "You have heard, have you not, of the tragic fate that has been foretold for the vast continent of Lemuria? Tell me, why can't we prevent this from happening? Our priests should be able to intervene. Surely we have the power and the technology. I cannot stand for us to just sit back, do nothing, and allow Lemuria to be destroyed. It's absolutely crazy, the poor Lemurians are probably counting on us to save them. I spent most of last night arguing with the other Makers trying to get them to intervene."

"Davodd," Namuani interposed, trying to soothe him. "You know, as well as I, that the Nine have decreed that the Lemurians have reached their time of completion. It is not up to us to alter the workings of destiny."

"Look, I'll tell you something that I have never told anyone," Davodd said with a trace of bitterness and anger edging into his voice. "Once, several years ago, I broke into the Crystal Hall of Records. You recall how rebellious I used to be. I wanted to see the secret information that is stored there on my family lineage and levels of attainment. I needed to know if I had a chance of becoming a Maker or not. Maybe they considered me too incorrigible. You know what I discovered that night, Nami? I learned that I had a sister in Atlantis whom I had never known. She was living in the Temple of Oralin. I didn't dare to approach her directly, but I saw her on a few occasions from a distance and I listened carefully lest I might hear anything spoken about her."

"Know I this kinswoman of yours?" questioned Namuani with astonishment.

"Possibly you might have heard of her, although she has not lived in Atlantis for many years. Her name is Diandra and it was she who was chosen to be sent to Lemuria as bride of their High King Altazar. Oh Nami, it has long been my desire to one day meet her; she is my only relative who remains. And now she is doomed with all of Lemuria to this horrible fate. What I cannot believe is that our cowardly priesthood is afraid to do anything about preventing this unnecessary tragedy. It's the same old stupid excuse of *not interfering with destiny.*" His voice crackled with cutting sarcasm.

"Davodd, I am truly sorry for the both of you," Namuani sympathized, "but my dear friend, you must know that life is transitory. We are birthed here, we live our lives to the best of our abilities, we learn, we serve, and finally we die in order to return to spirit and are born once again into the endless cycle. If you cannot know your sister this time around and if you have that strong desire, you will simply meet her during some other lifetime. You know Davodd, that all of what we term 'lifetimes' are just part of the one life of our soul's journey. Believe me, it saddens me greatly, that the Motherland will soon be gone from this Earth, but we must have faith and trust in the Greater Plan, though often we are unable to see it clearly in the light of its totality. Understand that the Higher Purpose is often beyond the breadth of our limited understanding, though sometimes we think that we know so much." She gently took his hand in hers.

Roughly pushing her away, Davodd snarled, "You are just as weak and complacent as all the others. Well, I am not going to just sit around mouthing spiritual platitudes while my sister is dying. She needs my help and somehow I will help her, even if the rest of her people will not." Davodd jumped up and stalked away.

Sighing, Namuani sadly let him go. There was nothing more that she could do for him, as much as she wanted to help him. Calling forth her children, they quickly departed.

That evening she reclined with the majestic head of the Master Vanel resting in her lap, stroking his shaggy dark curls while telling him of what had transpired during the day.

"Davodd is still quite the rebel, part of him simply refuses to grow up and release all his pent up anger and frustrations. The rest of him contains such rare brilliance and promise. What a paradox! And what a terrible waste of a remarkable human being. Just think what he could achieve with his talents if he ever developed some control and surrendered his fiery will to the Will of God. Unfortunately, there is nothing that I can do for him. I could neither calm him nor help him to understand. I just hope that he does not get himself into some terrible trouble over this. Can you imagine, sneaking into the Crystal Hall of Records! Who else would have the audacity?" And in spite of herself, a small smile broke through the corners of her mouth.

"Ah my precious woman," Vanel replied gently, "your friend treads a dark and dangerous path. We both know that he contains far too many imbalances within his emotional body for the work that he is doing."

"But he is permitted to be a Maker because of his great genius," Namuani explained.

"Yes, he has an incredibly creative mind. But, my dear, if he has no respect for the wisdom of the Seven or for the authority of the Nine, then he should not be in a position where he is working with the intense powers that hold the potential to destroy all of Atlantis."

Namuani listened carefully to Vanel's deep soothing

tones. He was such a powerful man with a strong spirit, that although he was profoundly gentle and quiet, he emanated an aura of invincible wisdom and authority. She felt so warm and protected being around this man. She had certainly been blessed in this lifetime with both a strong, adoring father, albeit she did not see him often, and with this incredible man who understood her to the very fibers of her being and who showered her with loving support.

Namuani remembered the symbol which she had embroidered on the back of the white silk robe which she always wore while performing. It was a single pink rose in the fullness of flowering. She had chosen it in honor of Vanel who had caused her innermost rose to unfold and blossom. Leaning close to him, she kissed him tenderly on his forehead.

"You are right about Davodd, my love. I will speak to my father about him at the first opportunity."

Vanel smiled at Namuani's innate purity of heart. Pulling her close to him, he enveloped her tenderly in his massive arms.

CHAPTER FOURTEEN:
DAVODD'S PLAN

Underground in his private chamber within the House of the Makers, Davodd pondered the plight of his sister Diandra. He still could not believe that the Atlanteans would make no effort to save Lemuria. He laid the blame at the fact that many of his people secretly looked down on the Lemurians as inferior to themselves. They were thought to be too emotional, too willful, too primitive to be equals of the spiritually refined, technologically advanced Atlanteans. Of course, that was what the Atlanteans criticized about him too, maybe he secretly contained some Lemurian blood.

Suddenly Davodd's keen, searching intellect found the solution that he had been seeking. His thoughts raced ever faster. "Could I do it? Dare I attempt it? Do I have sufficent knowledge?" Davodd felt the thrill of a challenge tingle throughout his brain.

Leaping up with excitement, Davodd left his chamber. He departed the House of the Makers through the system of underground tunnels, a maze of passageways which turned this way and that. Myriad intersections forced him to stop and focus on his intuition clearly. He began walking with a sure step and a steady purpose. Davodd knew not how he would do what he had now pledged to accomplish, but that somehow he would.

Finally he could see the dim glow of deep indigo light coming from the end of the passageway he followed. He was almost at his destination. The tunnel slanted up-wards and soon emerged outside. Here the air was charged with electrical currents of powerful forces. He took care with each step to remain directly in the center of the path. It wound its way up the side of the hill and stopped directly in front of a black, highly polished marble wall.

Davodd stopped here perplexed. "Now I need the password to enter through this wall and I know it not." Pulling a long thin key crystal from his robe, he pointed it at the wall, saying something that sounded like, *"Aztlan-Inra."* Davodd walked straight ahead into the wall and knocked his head against the hard stone surface.

"Owwwwww!" he exclaimed, rubbing his forehead. "Well, it is obvious that the password for the golden gate does not work on this wall. I must discover the correct words." He tried several different combinations, each time raising his crystal and stepping full of authority towards the wall until he crashed into it again and again. Davodd felt tears of frustration and anger begin to wet his eyes.

"I've got to get through this wall soon. I've wasted enough time as it is."

He set his mind to searching, scanning his problem from every intricate angle possible. "Even without knowing the password, there has to be a way to circumvent the entire process," he thought. Then he remembered some of the experimental research that he had done on the power of sound. "Yes, that is the secret! I just have to find a sound that acts as a master key, a vibration that will unlock any door," he exulted, knowing that he had almost discovered the answer.

Sitting down, Davodd totally stilled his being as he had been trained to do. His heartbeat became slower and slower, his breathing subsided and he entered a state of absolute quiet. He sat there lost in the great Silence . . . . Then it came, very quietly it came—at first it was a tiny whisper lost on the wind. He couldn't discern it clearly. Then louder and louder it became until it was the only sound he had ever known. It filled his entire being, that echoing, resounding sound until at last, there was no separation between him and the sound. He became the sound.

Finally Davodd opened his mouth slowly, opened his throat widely and gave birth to the sound. His entire body vibrated in harmony to the wave patterns of the sound, *his sound,* as his voice proclaimed it aloud. Then standing up, Davodd walked straight through the wall.

Inside all was bathed in a bright yellow light. Davodd stood still, listening to a steady hum emanating from something inside the room. He suddenly hoped that no one else was here. Up until now he hadn't dared to consider the possibility of what would happen to him if he were discovered in this secret place unbidden. Icy pangs of coldest fear took possession of his body, sending forth great shivers that turned his insides watery. He waited, yet felt no other presence.

Looking up, Davodd noticed a tall crystal pyramid atop the chamber. He recognized that the substance had been an invention of the Makers. His interest quickened when he saw in the center of the room a three-sided smaller pyramid located directly underneath the apex of the larger four-sided one.

"That has to be it; now where do I begin?"

Davodd had now calmed his fear sufficiently to set off exploring the perimeters of the room. He spotted a control panel built into the wall which looked like a large slab of crystal with a dial on the right side. As he inserted his crystal into a small hole at the top, symbols immediately began flashing across the face of the rock, ever changing, like a mirage. "I have activated it!" He suddenly felt a flush of confidence while remembering that he had worked on a crude prototype of this years before. Trying to remember the process, he began by setting the dial to the symbol for Lemuria, then Arnahem in particular, and sure enough, the same symbols soon appeared on the rock face. Davodd's cheeks blushed crimson with excitement as he entered in Diandra's name and her personal symbol flashed into view.

"Now I must be careful, very careful," he cautioned himself. He knew well that the slightest mistake would have disastrous consequences.

Moving to the three-sided pyramid, Davodd ascertained that it was truly empty save for the large chunk of smoky quartz. Then he carefully closed the chamber's glass door. Returning to the control panel he pressed the lever marked VACUUM. A great suctioning noise could be heard within the smaller pyramid. Then he placed his crystal into the ACTIVATE 1 slot. Lights flashed, causing the symbols upon the rock to rapidly change colors. Next the crystal was moved into ACTIVATE 2 position. This caused the center pyramid to glow a deep ruby red. Davodd felt his body begin to shake uncontrollably.

"Please, please, let me do this correctly," he pleaded. His trembling hand moved the crystal into ACTIVATE 3.

At once all the lights in the room were extinguished. Nothing could be seen except for the dimly flickering symbols on the stone in front of him and the deep redness of the pyramid. Even the hum had ceased.

"Oh no, I've done something wrong! I've ruined it. I've probably killed her. No, no!" he sobbed. "Diandra, please forgive me. I'm sorry, I'm so sorry."

Davodd's knees crumpled and he sank to the floor despairing that he had ever dared to come here. His cries wracked the silence, until, spent at last, he lay deep in silent grief. This pitiful man was so locked into his tragic error that it took him a while to notice that the hum had returned and the lights were flickering their way back to normal. Davodd was touched by the terrible fear of the awesome forces that he had just tampered with.

Glancing at the center pyramid he noticed that the redness had gone. Getting up, Davodd began those dreaded steps towards it, keeping his eyes averted, frightened of what he might see or not see. He approached the door and stopped, shutting his eyes tightly. Now he must take full responsibility for what he had wrought. Taking a deep breath, he uttered a short prayer and opened his eyes.

Inside the pyramid . . . .

. . . . . was the fragile form of a woman. Her hands were pressed tightly to her temples. Her eyes were open but saw not. Her face bore an expression of agony; she did not move.

"Oh God! Help us!" Davodd screamed as he flung open the door and tried to gather the rigid form of Diandra into his arms. He could not move her save lift her head up slightly and push back the masses of blond hair from her face. "I'm sorry Diandra, I'm sorry . . . Oh God, what have I done?" His voice choked with raw emotion.

"WHO DARES TO TRESPASS HERE?" thundered a voice filled with righteous wrath which cut through Davodd like a laser beam.

Davodd looked up through his tears and saw, *Oh No!*, the terrifying formidable figure of Dr. Z. looming before him in his deep blue ceremonial robes.

Then all was blackness . . . .

CHAPTER FIFTEEN:
THE CRYSTAL SURGERY

The world was spinning wildly. The excruciating pain throbbed with an unrelenting fierceness. It was as if hundreds of daggers stabbed and twisted and never let up.

The cry of Davodd shrieked across the horizon. "I'm sorry! Oh God, I'm sorry! Forgive me, Diandra! I have learned my lesson; I will never break the Law again! Forgive me, please!"

Then silence . . . . silence as still as death itself. For Davodd, it was a merciful silence. The pain had finally ripped him apart from his physical form and he knew no more of this world. He had been cursed to live again and again stripped of all knowledge, of all memories, until that day would dawn far into the future when the remembering would return and he would be tested once more.

*   *   *   *   *

For Diandra, the pain remained. She had been taken into Oralin, the Temple of the Creative Healing Wisdom, and placed in a small chamber filled with the emerald green ray of healing. Alorah stood close by her side with an aura of deep concern. Opposite her stood Dr. Z., his face grave. They had been laboring over her for hours. Nay, it had been days—days and nights without nourishment or sleep—just trying to pull Diandra out from her hellish nightmare place of paralyzing pain.

She moved now. Violent, jerky, uncontrolled movements as she thrashed about on the pallet. Low moans and half screams of terror escaped her parched lips. Alorah looked over to Dr. Z. He nodded his head to her with weary understanding. So far nothing had brought Diandra out of this state. There was but one thing left to try; this they both knew. The last hope, the ultimate process which they always sought to avoid unless all else had failed. It was the Crystal Surgery.

Alorah personally prepared Diandra. Removing her coverings, she began to apply an ointment to her naked body composed of pulverized gold and lapis lazuli among other highly secret ingredients. Attendants held down Diandra's twitching limbs until the task was completed. Then she lay still at last, falling deeply into a trance state, her body covered in a paste of sparkling blueness.

Dr. Z. had placed a pouch containing the appointed crystal upon a small altar. He was lost in concentration as he began his invocation. This crystal was so extremely powerful that it was kept buried in a hidden place except for the rare occasions when it was needed. Only the High Priestess Alorah and Dr. Z. held the authority and full knowledge to use it properly. The crystal was carefully unwrapped by Alorah and placed within a carved amethyst bowl while Dr. Z. intoned the necessary prayers. Then Dr.

Z. carefully picked up the crystal and held it aloft in both hands.

It was quite unlike any other crystal. The base which was heavy and wide contained small rocks of sparkling black set with tiny red crystals. Also fused into it were pebbles of purest white. The six sides of this double terminated crystal focused into the sharpest of points at one end, while the opposite end had multiple points. The interior itself was unfathomable; small prisms appeared and vanished into the changing mists of numerous dimensions. Its primary color was a transparent pale golden yellow. Yes, this crystal was capable of multiple functions which revealed themselves only after one had been initiated into its mysteries.

Dr. Z. held the crystal high above him. He delicately sought within himself for the correct usage of the crystal for Diandra. Beginning at her feet, he moved it up her body carefully, never actually touching her with the crystal. It was of utmost importance that he remain fully attuned to the balance of energy, if he gave her too much voltage from the crystal, the damage would be severe and irrevocable.

(The hermit wishes to speak with you here if I may. I am not at liberty to reveal to you the exact form of the surgical process which is taking place. This form of healing should not be attempted by anyone save the highly evolved ones who already carry this knowledge. It is exceedingly dangerous in the hands of the uninitiated. I might add that a few of these rare crystals are still in existence upon this earth even in the present age. They shall be found and recognized by those who carry the knowledge for their proper usage. And possibly they shall be of great benefit to mankind at some future date.)

When Dr. Z. had finished, he again raised the crystal skyward, evermore continuing with his prayers and invocations. Then turning to Alorah he said, "She shall sleep now. Our work is complete. Diandra will awaken in about three days and only then shall we know the full extent of her healing." Dr. Z. departed silently to cleanse and secret the crystal.

Later that same morning, Dr. Z. knew that he must speak with his daughter Namuani before he finally allowed himself to rest. Now that his long vigil was over he could feel the fatigue begin to flood his body. He had gone past the point where he could recharge himself. He simply needed to sleep.

Entering the portals of the small Temple of Enora, his heart felt weighted down with the heavy tidings that he carried. He knew very well the closeness that his daughter and Davodd had shared.

First Dr. Z. sought out the Master Vanel and held a brief, hushed conversation with him. Next he found Namuani with her students in a small room immersed in the multilayered sounds of numerous bells and chimes. Her delicate face burst into a delighted smile at the sight of him. But as she read his thoughts, her expression turned to one of concern and she hurried to his side and embraced him warmly. Dr. Z.'s heart melted in tenderness as it always did when he was near her. Then Namuani led her father into a secluded inner courtyard.

"Please, sit down on this bench with me, Father, and tell me what is troubling you, if you will." She spoke softly while taking his hand into hers.

"My dear Nami... I am sorry to have to bring sad news to you, but you must know and I should be the one to tell you," he began seriously. "Your friend Davodd is dead. He was punished by the Brotherhood of the Seven for a serious transgression of the Law."

Namuani broke into tears. "How? ... Why? ... Father, please tell me what happened."

"A few nights ago—I can no longer follow clearly the passing of time—I think that it was about three nights ago. Forgive me for being so weary; I have not slept for many days. Anyway, your dear friend Davodd trespassed into the Temple of Teleportation. We know not how he entered it since he was not privy to its password. He must have devised some method of circumventing our safeguards. Once he got into the temple, he somehow managed to teleport the priestess Diandra to Atlantis from Lemuria. Why he did this, we still do not know."

"I have the answer to that, Father," Namuani replied breathing deeply to regain composure. "Davodd discovered that Diandra was his sister and he despaired that she was about to die along with the entire continent of Lemuria. It is ironic, is it not, that now that she is back in Atlantis, he is not. . . . . But tell me, what of Diandra? How is she faring?"

"In a sense Davodd did save her, for he caused her to be brought to Atlantis just at the very moment when Lemuria underwent massive volcanic explosions and broke apart, sinking far beneath the ocean." Dr. Z. looked penetratingly at Namuani. He noticed how profoundly shocked she was by all of this. With great tenderness, he continued. "That is correct, the Motherland has truly disappeared beneath the ocean and shall be known no more on this earth except within our memories & legends. It's amazing to realize that it has totally gone. I fervently hope that Atlantis never suffers the same fate. But I sense that it could someday happen here as well. Everything is subject to change and to rising and falling. There is a lesson and a warning in this for all of us. . . " His voice trailed off as he became lost in deep thought.

"But Father," Namuani interjected after a few quiet moments, "please finish telling me what happened to Davodd and Diandra?"

"Unfortunately, Davodd knew not the entire procedure for the teleportation process. Far worse than that, Diandra was given no foreknowledge or preparation for the impending teleportation. So she was forcibly yanked from one world to another without her consent, so to speak. It is incredible that she survived at all. But that she did, although she suffers from unbelievable torments of pain and has not yet regained consciousness. Alorah and I just completed Crystal Surgery on her."

Namuani's eyes widened at the implications of what he had just said, "It is that serious?" she commented.

"Yes, it is, I'm afraid," her father answered solemnly. "Diandra will sleep for a few days more. When she awakens we shall know the full extent of the permanent damage to her."

Namuani cried quietly, holding her father closely to her. "I feel so sad about Davodd. Vanel and I both felt that something ominous was about to happen to him. I tried to find you to talk to you about him for the past three days, but no one seemed to know your whereabouts. Oh Father, if only this could have been prevented. It's hard for me to believe that we shall never see Davodd again." She cried and cried onto her father's shoulder making his robes quite wet with her tears.

"I'm truly sorry that I have had to bring such heavy tidings to you, Nami." Dr. Z. felt as if he, himself, might break into tears soon. This daughter of his was the only one who he allowed to open up the fortress of his emotions.

Vanel silently entered the courtyard and approached his wife, holding open his arms to her with loving understanding. "Come, my love, let your father get some rest." Namuani flung herself into his healing embrace while choking back her sobs.

Gratefully thanking the Master Vanel, Dr. Z. bid them both farewell and thus departed for his private place where he could finally find respite from his tremendous responsibilities. He wondered why he so frequently forgot that he was human like the other people, and often denied himself the human basics such as food and sleep. After the crisis had passed, only then, did he realize that he was near the point of collapse. He thus resolved to try to take better care of his physical form.

"This must be a sign that I have finally reached the point of aging, the stage where even prolonged immersion in the rejuvenation temples would only have a limited effect," he realized with bemused astonishment as he slowly made his way through the shining white streets of Atlantis.

***   ***   ***

Thus passed the fateful days when Lemuria met its doom and destiny was manipulated for Diandra. Lest you wish to forget these troubled times and ever be tempted to tamper with fate yourself, please remember the price that is always paid.

For Davodd . . . it was death and the loss of his vast intellect.

For Diandra . . . we shall see.

CHAPTER SIXTEEN:
THE MUSIC OF THE SPHERES

The music arced higher and higher until it soared past the two pillars that mark the gateway to this universe. Then the Music of the Spheres began a graceful curve, full of celestial resonance, spiraling into infinity. Fainter and fainter it became until that moment of return. Now it sounded different, containing traces of other-worldly melodies as it came closer. Louder it came, pulled once again towards the gravity of the earth until it anchored there with an endearing sweetness which washed over and through its listener while dissolving all barriers to her unshed tears. Then the tears fell in a relentless flood. They were the years of tears that had long been held back by discipline and denial. Diandra cried and cried from that lost place and it seemed as if the crying would never cease. Soon she realized that her tears were but the rain. She rained and rained experiencing one of the most perfect forms of release. Absolutely surrendering to it, she let go completely. In the letting go and in the flow of the music which surrounded her, Diandra finally knew peace. The pain stopped. The dizzy, screaming, throbing pain simply let go and was no more.

The beautiful Alorah stood by her side ever so patiently, radiating her starry presence with golden beams of dancing light. Monitoring Diandra, she carefully noted each nuance of what the woman was experiencing.

At last, when the storm had long ceased, the High Priestess touched Diandra lightly upon her forehead with a crystal of purest azurite. Diandra's breathing slowly began to even out. Then her eyes opened, still wet with tears. She knew not where she was. Looking fully into Alorah's starry orbs which contained the infinity of space, she began to cry once again. Alorah leaned forward and gently taking Diandra's hand in hers, kissed her forehead.

"Do not try to speak yet, Diandra," Alorah said firmly. "I am Alorah whom you have known since the Beginning. You have returned to your homeland of Aztlan." *(She spoke one of the secret names for Atlantis, knowing that it would have greater impact to penetrate Diandra's unconscious.)* "You must be very quiet and allow your senses to awaken gently."

Diandra nodded weakly and closed her eyes once more. The music awaited her still. She could see the stars rotating and shimmering—the whole universe turning in accompaniment to this wondrous music. Sinking deeper into the all-encompassing sounds, she felt her entire being drifting gently through the vastness of space. Diandra followed the notes of a flute which gracefully glided through the labyrinths of twisting constellations. Her entire world pulsated and turned; yet she lost not the flute sounds and let them guide her back.

"Back to where?" She heard herself thinking.

"Back home," came her answer.

"Which home?" she inquired.

"Your home on planet Earth," her mirror self replied.

"Where is my home?" questioned she in an etheric voice sounding so extremely detached and far away.

"Aztlan," replied herself, albeit a different self. This one seemed to know more than that other part of her.

"Who am I?" The question bubbled up from the bottom of an aqua sea. She saw iridescent fish swimming through the churning, foaming mist of bubbles and undulating underwater plants.

"Don't you know—don't you know—don't you know?" echoed her answering smart self.

"No, I know not," she said meekly.

"*I* know," she answered confidently.

"Who am I then? Please tell me. I'm getting so confused," she pleaded.

"Not yet-not yet-not yet—we must rest first," repeated the reply.

"I must know. Who am I?" She was floating further and further away. The song of the flute was fading into the distant void.

"Diandra! We are she," the voice exclaimed with authority.

"Ah, Diandra . . . I have heard that name before," she said softly in a voice filled with wonder.

"Diandra, follow the flute. It will return you to where you belong," she ordered herself.

As Diandra floated through the shifting heavens, she searched for the flute song. "It was just here. Now where did it disappear to? I must not lose it," she thought. Then she caught a note drifting lazily by her on a shaft of silvery moonlight. Reaching out her hand, she grabbed onto it, and it pulled her along skimming through the waves of the sky. More notes appeared until she could again discern the melody clearly. She held on to the music and let it take her with it until she experienced a sudden jarring sensation, a feeling of being locked into a tight space from which she was not allowed to escape.

"Relax now. Let it be. This is the place in which we belong," her other self explained.

So Diandra lay back and tried to settle in and find comfort within this confining form. She searched for the feeling of limitlessness within its limits.

"Diandra!"—She was being called again. This time there was a sense of urgency.

"How very strange this all is," she thought.

"Diandra, open your eyes!" the voice softly commanded.

"What are eyes?" She wanted to ask.

But before she could fully form the question, she answered, "You know what eyes are. You cannot go back out there into infinite space. It is no longer allowed. You must remain here in your body. Diandra, open your eyes!"

Slowly, with great effort, Diandra once again opened her eyes; they were so heavy that it took a large amount of concentration and will power to get them open. Light flooded in, making her blink rapidly in protection from its glare. In her instant of openness she saw that she was not alone. A man and a woman stared at her intently.

"Who are these people?" she wondered.

Alorah reached for her hand and reassured her. "I am Alorah. This is Dr. Z. You have returned to the continent of Aztlan."

"Oh yes, I almost remember," spoke Diandra in a wan voice as she closed her eyes and returned to sleep.

Alorah glanced sharply at Dr. Z. "Well, what do you think?" she asked him.

"Much better than I had expected," he replied in even, measured tones. "However, she is obviously having difficulties retrieving her memory. She is also reluctant to remain in her physical body, which is understandable due to the pain that she has experienced. This shall improve with time now that the pain has left her. We can also assume that most of her supra-normal abilities have been severely damaged. Do not allow yourself to be saddened by her condition, Alorah. It is far better than I believed possible." Dr. Z.'s voice was warm with compassion.

Alorah nodded mutely in agreement, her lovely, highly attuned, other-worldly face shadowed by her loving concern. She knew well that she could not waste her energy mourning what had now been lost, but must instead be grateful and work with what remained. Diandra was alive . . . and she lived without pain.

**** **** **** **** **** *****

Thus it was for Diandra. As the years passed by in Atlantis, she was cared for by the sisters of the Temple of Oralin. Most of her days were spent on the shoreline gazing at the distant western horizon of the Great Ocean. The sea birds grew so used to her presence that they became tame and would sit by her feet and on her shoulders. She learned to speak to them in their own language. *(We can only wonder what they communicated to each other.)* Fishermen began bringing the sick and injured birds to her, and in her own special way, she would heal them and set them free.

Diandra's full memory never returned nor did most of her conscious knowledge of the Mysteries until this present age. She spoke not of Altazar or Lemuria nor of her past. She turned increasingly inward in focus, emanating a soft silvery light. It was as if she lived within another dimension, a world that knew not pain and absence of love. She found great solace in observing the rising and falling of the blue waters of the Great Ocean. *(In truth, much of her consciousness had returned to her home, the great domed city of Daluum, floating within the currents of her watery planet of Arion. But that is for another story.)*

After a few years, Diandra withdrew herself yet further from temple life and was not heard to speak again to another human.

CHAPTER SEVENTEEN:
THE ENCHANTMENT

The giant condor circled high above them. Every feather upon him could be perfectly delineated due to the clarity of the air at this high altitude. Far below, his shadow played delicately upon the bleak landscape surrounding the temple complex at TI-WA-KU. There were few trees to provide shade from the sun's relentless strange blue rays which seemed to radiate simultaneous warmth and cold. Amidst the unending starkness, the shimmering blue waters of Lake Ti-Tika provided the sole note of freshness against mammoth mountains of dullest grey.

Altazar and Solana stood on its shore lazily casting nets for the small silver fishes which darted about its watery depths. They knew not how much time had elapsed since they had first arrived at TI-WA-KU. In this place, time did not exist in the usual sense. It could have been a short while or many years. Neither of them could measure it with any degree of accuracy although both of them had tried. TI-WA-KU lived in a reality separate from the rest of the known world.

Altazar seemed strangely content here. He no longer mentioned to Solana their mission to Atlantis. It was as if he had stepped out of the world and did not want to be reminded of it. He had grown quite close to the woman Mu'Ra and often shared her bed. She had long been involving him in numerous occult rituals and initiations into strange practices.

As always, Solana observed Altazar carefully and said little. A curious detachment was building between the two of them. Solana was concerned for his friend, who seemed to lose himself more and more as he allowed Mu'Ra to assume control over him—oblivious to where it might lead. Hence Solana watched and waited, searching for the clues he needed in order to fully understand the nature of the energies that were manifest here. He still distrusted the alien woman Mu'Ra, seeing her clearly as a powerful sorceress weaving subtle gossamer webs of magic around Altazar until finally she would take possession of his very soul. But he could speak not of this to Altazar, knowing well that this would only serve to turn his friend against him. *(A warning can only be effectively received when one is ready to hear it.)* Thus Solana maintained an air of friendly discretion while waiting patiently for the correct instant in which to act. He felt that since they had been here for such a long time, the opportunity would surely come soon.

Altazar pulled in his net which sparkled with the glints of several small fish. "See, my friend, this is how it is done. Mu'Ra will be pleased with us. Solana, you don't seem to have your heart in fishing today. What troubles you?"

Solana gave his friend a searching look and decided that this might be his chance to speak frankly with him.

"Altazar, let us sit for awhile. I wish to talk with you. Please spare me some of your attention and I will share my thoughts with you."

The High King sat down upon one of the rock steps which led down into the lake. Upon his face he wore an expression of puzzlement. "Speak Solana, and I will listen."

Taking a seat beside him, Solana searched for the right combination of words to reach Altazar. Beginning slowly, he said, "We have journeyed together for a long time, my dear brother. Who knows just how many years have passed since that distant morning when we set out from my homeland of Rapan-Nui on our great trek to Atlantis. Since we have been in TI-WA-KU, it appears as if time itself has stopped. However, I am sure that in the rest of the world, time surely continues its passing. It is certain that our travels have ceased. Do you remember that we were empowered by my priests on Rapan-Nui to go to Atlantis? I still carry upon me the messages that I was asked to deliver to the Brotherhood of the Seven. My people entrusted me with this important task, Altazar, and I am not fulfilling it. They also charged me with the responsibility of taking you safely to Atlantis. I am not keeping my promises. Maybe now you can understand why my heart is not at peace here when my duty still lies before me uncompleted. I understand that you are content and wish not to leave, but I know that the day must soon arrive when we go forward once again and discharge our duties."

Solana looked at Altazar anxiously, trying to discern his level of receptivity to what had been said. "What think you of my words?"

Altazar sighed deeply. This conversation made him

uncomfortable, but at the same time, he recognized the truth in it. "You are right, Solana. We must leave here sometime soon, although, I myself, do not really wish to go."

Solana felt a sense of cautious relief. "You can always return here later, after our travels to Atlantis are completed, if that is your desire."

"Yes, I am aware of that. But it will not be easy for me to leave Mu'Ra. I have grown unusually attached to her. However, I shall not seek to avoid the path of my duty. I shall speak to Mu'Ra about this tonight in her private chambers; hopefully, she will understand its importance and be understanding. When do you want to depart?" Altazar queried.

"As soon as possible . . . why not tomorrow?" answered Solana while thinking to himself, "If only she will let us go."

****
****

Later that evening in the woman's sleeping chambers, Altazar lay entwined in Mu'Ra's powerful naked limbs which were wrapped sinuously around him. Long ropes of her heavy black hair coiled around him like many writhing serpents. He had grown used to the solid weight of her body and the way that her need to possess seemed almost to devour him. Sometimes he actually felt smothered by her presence, as if fighting for a breath of fresh air. However, now that he had spent so much time with her he found himself developing a real need to experience that wild sensation of being taken over by her powerful magnetism. It helped him to forget himself and his sorrows.

Altazar stirred himself to speak. "My passionate puma,

I need to speak with you . . . " he began hesitantly, wondering why it felt so difficult to inform her of his leave-taking. *(He remembered that distant day when he had spoken to Diandra of his impending departure for Rapan-Nui and felt a pang of sweet sadness pulse through his heart. He had not wanted to leave Diandra then either— nor should I have—he thought bitterly.)* But he wondered why it was so hard for him to tell Mu'Ra now. "Am I afraid of her?" he questioned himself.

"Long ago, when I first arrived in TI-WA-KU," he began anew, "Solana and I were on our way to the continent of Atlantis. We had been sent there by our high priests on Rapan-Nui. In fact the very survival of the remnants of our people who survived may well depend on our obtaining some sort of aid for them from the Atlanteans. Instead of fulfilling our duty to the Motherland of Lemuria, we have allowed ourselves to be waylaid in TI-WA-KU, although it has been a most pleasant experience here for me." He kissed her on the cheek, not noticing the coldness that had settled into her expression.

"Anyway, the time has come for us to continue on our journey. After my task is completed, it is my strong desire to return here and be with you once again." Altazar glanced at Mu'Ra fondly, unaware of the sharp glints of anger in her stormy eyes. "Our plan is to leave here tomorrow and travel to the mysterious Kingdom of AN. I shall miss you greatly, you know."

There was silence. It was an ominous silence. The air felt charged with built-up pressure as if a volcano was about to explode. Altazar searched for what was wrong. "Was it something that I have said?" he wondered.

Suddenly Mu'Ra sat bolt upright on the sleeping platform and shrieked, "HA!" Leaping to a standing position, she grew taller and even more imposing as if drawing unseen powers into herself.

She growled, "YOU DARE! YOU DARE! YOU FOOL! Who cares about your petty problems? Lemuria is gone! You will never leave here alive. You are MINE! You belong totally to me and do not ever think otherwise, YOU STUPID FOOL! No one ever leaves me. NO ONE! I am the LAST!"

"Tell me, why are you the last, Mu'Ra? Why did the others leave you here alone when they returned to their place of origin?" Altazar asked in a controlled, even tone, masking his surprise at her outburst.

"Because they accused me of becoming too powerful. They were afraid of me. They didn't think that I was pure enough for them! And they wouldn't allow me to return with them when our work here was finished. They left me here all ALONE when they abandoned this place. Now I am stuck here on this wretched planet without my people." Mu'Ra's rage suddenly changed into a dry bitterness. At the same time her face was changing rapidly from young to old, beautiful to ugly, to a horrifying alien being that Altazar had never seen in her before.

He watched this spectacle calmly, both fascinated and repelled by her. "You've been here alone ever since they left you?" he inquired with some sympathy.

"No, you fool." Her voice turned mocking. "I know how to get myself a man when I need one. If he comes within one hundred leagues of TI-WA-KU I can draw him here with my magic, as I did with you."

"What happened to the other men that you brought here? Where are they?" Altazar asked with a rising sense of dread.

"They were sent to the parallel dimensions after I had finished with them," Mu'Ra snarled, then noticing the look of shock and revulsion on Altazar's face, she added, "Do not look so concerned, my pet. They were happy here with me. I taught them much that they could not have learned elsewhere—like you." She smiled at him affectionately. "None of them complained. They begged me to possess them like you do, dear Altazar. I help to heal your pain, don't I?"

Mu'Ra turned herself into a seductress, the most alluring woman he had ever encountered. She began slinking towards him while waves of compelling magnetism encircled his being. Approaching him, she lingered close enough to slowly, sensuously draw one of her long tapered fingers down his face and chest, shooting thunderbolts of desire flaming throughout Altazar's senses.

"Go away," Altazar muttered through clenched teeth. "Let me go!" He pushed her hand away fiercely.

"Altazar, you know that you will *never* be able to leave me," she purred as she began rubbing her body caressingly against his.

Then Altazar knew that he had no choice. There would be no escape from this woman. He could not, would not, leave TI-WA-KU. He had been caught in a trap of enchantment. He had blindly walked himself right into it. Now he understood the purpose of all their strange rituals. They had bound his soul. Finally he could see it all clearly; his awareness had returned. But, alas, it was too late. The bonds had already been tightened. He was no longer the keeper of his destiny. He belonged to her.

With a low groan escaping his broken heart, Altazar forcibly pulled Mu'Ra into his arms and carried her to the sleeping platform.

CHAPTER EIGHTEEN:
THE CONFRONTATION

Early in the morning the storm came. Thunderous bolts of lightning lit up the pre-dawn darkness with an awesome display of sheer raw energy. It was as if the Gods themselves flexed their mighty power, unleashing the memory of their omnipotence over the smallness of man. *(Must not mankind be continually reminded of how little control over nature he actually possesses?)* Then the rains came. Torrents of giant-sized raindrops pelted the parched earth and could not soak into the dry soil. They formed trickles which turned into streams that ran together and flooded everything that lay within their path to the lake. There they experienced the release of their union into the frothy, storm-tossed waters of Lake Ti-Tika.

Altazar had slept not. A sense of tragic resignation had swept over him. He had failed once more and was no longer worthy to be deemed a High King. How many times had he let down his people? How could he have been so overwhelmingly blind as to have let Mu'Ra entrap him in such a debasing way? He paced the main temple, ignoring the presence of the ever-present four spirit/guards stationed, as usual, one at each direction. How could he face Solana ever again, he anguished. Solana had not been bewitched. He probably had been aware of his possession by Mu'Ra ever since it first began. A sense of great shame and embarrassment, of overriding guilt shook his soul.

"How could I have been so foolish?" he despaired. "I lost myself and now I cannot escape her." Thinking back to the night just passed and to their savage passion, he loathed himself for all his weaknesses. He yearned to be able to cut himself free and depart this treacherous place with Solana, but he could not. When he tried to move himself in that direction, it was as if his energy was blocked. He could not budge. No, he was mired here by some dark spell that he himself had participated in, that he knew not how to undo. Altazar was thoroughly revulsed at himself.

"Good morning, Altazar. Well my friend, are you ready to depart?" Solana had just entered with that graceful lightness to his step. He wore his magenta poncho with the conch shell from AN dangling proudly around his neck.

Altazar hung his head and dropped his gaze to the floor, unable to bring his dishonored self to look at Solana's bright clarity. Of course, all that Solana need do was but glance at him, reading Altazar's energy, and feel his sense of disgrace and shame. Tears came quickly then to Solana's eyes as he reached out to Altazar and embraced him firmly. He felt Altazar's pain and discomfort, and above all else, his guilt for having failed so many. Still Altazar would not look upon his friend.

Holding Altazar tightly by his shoulders, Solana's eyes misted with compassion and forgiveness. "It is all right, dear brother. I understand what has befallen you. Would that I could undo the spell which binds you but I cannot. My knowledge is not strong in such areas. At least your awareness of your situation has returned. If you can hold on to that, a day may come when the door to your freedom shall stand open for you. I will pray for that."

Altazar stood mutely listening, staring blankly at the floor, still too ashamed to meet Solana's steady gaze.

"I would remain here with you if I could," Solana continued. "But you know, as well as I, the importance of completing our mission. Therefore I shall go for the both of us. Somehow I will make it all the way to Atlantis. This must be done. My heart is grieved to leave you, my dearest of friends. If only we had arrived at the Kingdom of AN rather than this bewitched place. But then, who am I to question the workings of destiny? Try to be content, Altazar. Remember that you have been happy here, maybe you can be again. Please do not burden yourself with guilt. What has been done is past. There are reasons for all the baffling things that happen to us that sometimes appear 'negative.' It is simply that we don't have the full understanding to see them in their proper perspective, in their place in the wholeness of the greater Plan."

"We create our future by our thoughts and actions right now in this present moment. When you realize this, you will be able to free yourself from this situation." Solana closed his eyes and let fall his hands from Altazar's shoulders. "Farewell, Altazar," said he and turned to depart.

"Wait a minute, you are not going anywhere!" A foreboding shadow loomed in the open doorway. Mu'Ra stepped inside smiling sweetly, fingering a slender silver dagger whose hilt was inlaid with the palest of blue turquoise.

Solana hesitated, eying the dagger with caution. "Altazar remains here with you, Mu'Ra. You have no further use for me. I shall not be returning to TI-WA-KU. Please step aside that I may depart."

"*No one* ever leaves here. I have told you that. What makes you think that you are the exception to my decree? I am the Last," she said very softly with only the most subtle of threats in her velvety voice.

"I must go, hence I shall go, so you may call me the First!" Solana said, radiating authority in a voice which Altazar had never before heard him use.

"So you imagine. HA! Do not mimic me, you fool!" She stroked her shiny dagger lovingly.

Altazar stood watching all of this as if it were a dream. Standing between the two of them, he felt the tug of their energies upon him as if caught in the middle between two magnetic poles. Wishing that Mu'Ra would let Solana leave, he fervently hoped that Solana would not be harmed. He wanted desperately to go too, but he had lost his personal power and will; he could do nothing unless that temptress decreed it. She had his energy tightly locked up in her grip. All that he could do was to passively stand by and watch this terrible drama unfold, knowing that somehow he had caused all this trouble.

"So you think that you can overpower me, do you Solana?" Mu'Ra taunted. "And you think that Altazar is your loyal friend, do you? Well, I will show you which of us is the stronger and I'll show you how low your exalted High King of Lemuria has fallen."

Solana stood his ground with a quiet firmness, never flinching from her cruel gaze.

"Altazar, come to me, my dearest," she cooed in her low sultry voice. "I have something special for you."

Altazar tried not to move, willed himself not to move, but instead found himself walking towards her. "Yes, my tigress, what do you wish of me?" came out of his lips while inside himself he was pleading, "Please give me control of myself. Do not let me be used by this evil woman."

"Now kiss me and stroke me in front of your friend," she commanded silkily.

Not daring to look at Solana, Altazar found himself taking Mu'Ra into his arms and kissing her passionately. One of his hands slipped inside her tunic and caressed her breast.

"There, that's enough!" She laughed mockingly and pushed him rudely away. "Do you like my big pussycat, Solana, or would you like to see more?"

Altazar reddened with shame and suppressed anger while Solana watched it all calmly and spoke not a word.

Mu'Ra glared with open hatred at Solana. "So you think that you're so full of perfect control, do you?" She handed the silver dagger to Altazar saying, "Here, my pet, now go and kill your friend."

Altazar glanced dumbly at the dagger in his hand. Its sharp silvery shining seemed to call out for blood. He felt its energy begin to intoxicate him like a drug. His blood began coursing rapidly through his veins. "I must obey, I must obey," sang his blood. "I must kill Solana now," it commanded.

He took a few tentative steps towards Solana. He raised the dagger in his hand. His dazed eyes, full of the torments of his deep inner conflict, met the pure green of Solana's unflinching stare. Altazar paused, then slowly drew that instrument of death ever closer to Solana's heart. Very carefully, Solana raised the conch shell to his lips and blew a long steady note.

Time froze for an instant. Then that instant passed. Altazar strengthened his grip for the death blow. But Solana was gone. He had simply vanished.

A fierce cry arose from the imprisoned depths of Altazar. "What have I done?" he screamed. Turning around wildly, he ran to Mu'Ra and plunged the dagger deeply into her chest.

Mu'Ra fell lifeless unto the floor. Altazar glanced around him quickly, still in a frenzy. The spirit/men turned a sickly pale blue as they faded into oblivion. A deep sob burst forth from Altazar's throat as he ran from the temple into the pelting rain. He ran past the steps to the lake, running blindly with no direction. He stumbled and ran until he could run no more.

**** * ***** * *****

Thus it was, that dark and stormy day at the Temple of TI-WA-KU. The heavens themselves opened up with their anguish as Altazar fell so deeply from grace. And hence it was that Solana was nearly betrayed by his friend and that they were duly parted.

I cried on that day. I grieved for the both of them. I wept, knowing how difficult it would be for Altazar to forgive himself and become whole again. First he would have to release the enormous guilt that he had taken upon himself. Only then could he begin to remember the truth and join me on the Crystal Mountain.

CHAPTER NINETEEN:
THE KINGDOM OF AN

When Solana had blown upon his conch shell trumpet back in the Temple of TI-WA-KU he had no idea of what it might do. That moment had been fraught with so much danger, he had simply followed the message of his inner voice to sound the shell. He had watched Altazar's final debasement with detached disbelief, hoping that by letting the drama play itself out, it would serve to break Altazar free. Unfortunately, it did not, or so he thought. For when the conch responded to his breath with its long deep call, everything disappeared from sight.

Solana found himself standing alone, unharmed, high atop a mountain. He knew not where he was nor how he had gotten there. Far away in the distance he could see a small patch of undulating blue water and assumed that it was probably part of Lake Ti-Tika. He was now far above the tree line and the extremely high altitude gave the air a crystal clarity which charged it with vital force or *prana-chita*. He could see little diamonds dancing about in the atmosphere surrounding him. Wherever he was, he knew not, but it filled him with wonder.

Solana stood facing the Sun and raised his arms to it, gratefully reciting the ancient prayer to AN.

> *Reverence to thee, O AN of ANTES!*
> *Thou art the eye of the storm,*
> *The light in the darkness,*
> *The darkness within the light.*
>
> *Grant me, O mighty AN*
> *That I may walk a path of peace,*
> *That I may embody your wholeness,*
> *For I am just and true.*

When he had finished, he sat down, arranging the folds of his poncho around him, and began to meditate.

After meditating for some time, he became conscious of the sound of gently tinkling bells approaching him. Opening his eyes, Solana noticed a man coming towards him carrying a golden staff capped by a gold Sun and Moon from which dangled several tiny golden bells. The stranger had a face of immense nobility and carried himself with a certain regal splendor. He was tall with loose black hair and an extremely handsome face. His strong dark eyes were deep and kind. A short tunic of finely woven alpaca wool was worn on his lean body. Most remarkably, in his ears were huge golden ear plugs fashioned into glowing Sun discs.

The stranger bowed to him then raised his arms sunward. "Solana, we welcome you to the Kingdom of AN!" he announced proudly. "My name is Aka-Capac. Come with me and I shall lead you there."

Solana smiled broadly, first with relief at his deliverance, then with the great joy of anticipation. He had found the Kingdom of AN! Standing up, he clasped Aka-Capac's hand firmly. "Thank you for finding me. Please lead the way and I shall follow!"

Aka-Capac looked at him with warmth and understanding; then he, too, smiled joyously and nodded. "Come brother, you have been through much today. Soon you shall find rest."

He led the way down the mountainside following a small, but well-maintained trail. They slowly picked their way down the steep slopes zig-zagging back and forth along the face of the mountain. Down below, Solana could see a river winding its way through a fertile green valley.

"Is that AN?" he asked

Aka-Capac responded, "It is indeed AN and so is this and so are we." He gestured to the mountains and sky all around them.

After some time they descended to the valley floor and hiked along the banks of the river for several miles. Soon the sound of distant music could be heard—just a waft on the fresh breeze. Then, as they came closer, the long low rumbling of a horn could be heard from a nearby peak. It echoed throughout the valley. Then another horn seemed to answer it from a different mountain further away.

"They announce our approach now," Aka-Capac explained.

Solana felt a profound sense of excitement well up inside of him. Soon they passed through two giant boulders which marked the entrance to the hidden valley of Ani. Several men who bore a strong family resemblance to Aka-Capac stood on guard and waved to them as they walked by.

Aka-Capac turned to Solana and whispered to him, "Now blow upon your conch shell once again and send your salutations to AN."

Solana straightened himself and with great seriousness and respect put the conch to his lips and blew. The sound flew swiftly on the wind like a golden arrow. Then there could be heard the answering echoes-echoes-echoes bouncing from mountain to mountain until they faded softly away.

Aka-Capac grinned at him, "Well done, brother. Welcome home, Solana. It is indeed an honor to bring you here."

As they walked onwards with bouncy strides, Solana saw houses of stone with roofs of thatched grass tucked here and there. And there were people! Beautiful, healthy looking men, woman, and children who waved and smiled at them as they passed by.

Excited whispers could be heard, "Look, there is Solana. He has come. Solana has made it home!" Everywhere there was an atmosphere of love and friendliness.

Ahead of them loomed a large step pyramid made of sun-baked bricks of earth atop stones. "This is the Pyramid of Anani," Aka-Capac told him. "Our Ancient Ones await us here. Are you ready to greet them?" he asked.

"Yes," replied Solana humbly. He felt as if his heart would burst with sheer joy and elation any moment now. "AN is just as I always imagined it to be," he explained to Aka-Capac. "It is so perfectly familiar here."

"That is simply because this is the home of your true lineage. It is ever that way for those of us returning here for the first time. We have all dreamt of this place, but were never quite certain if AN existed on the physical plane or not," said Aka-Capac.

They had now arrived at the base of the Pyramid of Anani and began ascending the endless stairs which climbed up the front of it until they reached what could be termed the fourth level.

Entering through an inclined angular doorway, they found themselves in a large square room. Seated within, upon chairs exquisitely fashioned of silver and gold, were a man and a woman who were the most fascinating beings that Solana had ever seen. Clad simply in white tunics, they were old, incredibly old, but glowed with the radiant beauty of their shining, transcendent essences. They emanated Perfect Love and Purest Wisdom.

Solana had a strong sensation that he knew these two very well indeed. He experienced an overwhelming sense of nostalgia poised on the edge of full remembrance.

"Solana, is it you?" the man asked in a voice containing utmost authority.

"Yes, *Tayta* . . . Father, Father of the Sun," responded Solana with strong emotion as the man wrapped him in an embrace.

"Solana, my son, we are pleased to welcome you home to the Kingdom of AN," spoke the Father-Sun.

The woman stood patiently waiting to greet Solana. Her snowy white hair was pulled back and plaited into a loose knot. Her face, though well wrinkled with age, shone with a joyful beauty. Taking Solana into her arms at last, she held him closely and whispered.

"Oh Solana, we welcome you to AN. Long have we awaited this day, watching you draw ever closer. We have never doubted that you would find your way here," she said quietly with deep emotion.

"*Mamay*, Mother of the Moon . . . oh *Mamaki*!" Solana

responded with gentle tenderness, never questioning how he recognized them or knew their names, or why he dared to address them so familiarly.

"You must both be tired and hungry from your lengthy travels, are you not?" she inquired. Turning to one of their attendants, she motioned that food might be brought for Solana and Aka-Capac. They were led into a nearby alcove, whereupon they seated themselves comfortably on large woven cushions on the floor. Here they were served most wondrous food and drink that left Solana feeling quite refreshed and renewed.

After they had eaten their fill, the Father-Sun asked, "But what has happened to Altazar? Was he not to travel here with you?"

Solana's bright face clouded over in sorrow at the memories of his dear friend. "That is a most sad story. I'm afraid that he is lost to us. On our way here, we were captured and taken to the Temple of TI-WA-KU. There he suffered an enchantment by Mu'Ra of the four-fingered ones. I could not bring him here with me. Mu'Ra would not even permit me to depart. Finally she commanded Altazar to stab me with her silver dagger. He was about to kill me when I was told by an inner voice to blow upon the conch." Solana gestured to the shell hanging from the woven strap around his neck. "I wonder if there is not some way that we could make haste and rescue him from that demented sorceress?" he implored.

"Solana, my dear," the Mother-Moon replied firmly with her far-seeing wisdom, "we cannot interfere into the affairs of TI-WA-KU, nor can they interfere with us. Back in the ancient of days long ago, it was peopled by many of the four-fingered ones, starry beings, many of whom originated from the Sirian System. They were some of the earliest colonists upon this planet. TI-WA-KU functioned then as an important center of initiation and learning for mankind."

"Our earliest legends tell that back at the beginning of this earth cycle there was a sacred cave with four openings. This cave was located not far from the shores of Lake Ti-Tika. From each of these openings there emerged a man and woman who were brother/sister as well as mates. These four brothers were called Ra'Mu, Me'Ru, Ma'Nu, and Ra'Ma. The sister of the one known as Ra'Mu was the original Mu'Ra."

She continued, "Many of the ancestors of numerous tribal groups and kingdoms were fathered by those beings at TI-WA-KU from the distant universes. Know you not that they were the forefathers of your own people on Rapan-Nui and Lemuria? We ourselves, carry their blood in our lineage. Therefore TI-WA-KU will always be a sacred ancestral shrine to us regardless of who is living there. Remember the star beings who inhabited that place were highly evolved ones who came to this planet to serve humankind. Many useful things were introduced to the people by them: methods of agriculture, cosmology, weaving, telepathic processes, sacred knowledge of metals and crystals, herbal lore and leverage of stones—wondrous things too numerous to mention which were of great benefit to the planet."

"What happened to the original inhabitants of TI-WA-KU?" Solana inquired with great fascination.

"The cycle for their work here simply completed itself," the Father-Sun answered. "Hence they departed this planet and returned to the galactic systems from whence they originated."

"All save one," Aka-Capac added in his deep voice. "The sorceress Mu'Ra was not permitted to return with the others because her energies had become too poisoned by contact with the density of the earth's magnetic field."

"Understand, Solana," Mother-Moon continued knowledgeably, "what happened was that the woman Mu'Ra allowed her auric shield to be penetrated by contact with too many earth men who had, of course, lower energy frequencies than the star beings. This in turn lowered hers until she no longer had the impeccable integrity and control which is an absolute prerequisite in order to be a pure channel for the higher dimensional energies. Mu'Ra could no longer handle them in the correct way so she increasingly turned to magic and manipulation as an outlet for release of the immensely powerful frequencies to which her being was accustomed."

"Thus her energies became increasingly distorted," explained Aka-Capac.

"Why did this not happen to the others of her kind as well?" Solana asked.

Mother-Moon explained, "Because although it is not harmful for a star being man to plant his star seed within an earth woman, it is an entirely different matter when the situation is reversed. The four-fingered women were informed of the hazards to their energy fields should they become sexually involved with an earthly man. The other women followed these guidelines, Mu'Ra did not. She even transgressed to the degree that she gave birth to several children by different human men. This definitely caused a severe disturbance to her dimensional polarities."

(The unusual histories of the children of Mu'Ra would make a fascinating story in itself, if the hermit had but the time to remember.)

"What I still do not understand is this," interjected Solana. "If AN is aware of all this, why do you choose to do nothing about her?"

The Father-Sun now spoke with calm authority. "Because, Solana, AN holds an ancient pact of trust with TI-WA-KU which presupposes noninterference and mutual respect. Thus it is out of our sphere of influence to intercede, even though, sadly enough, it has now become a focus of negative energy patterns."

"Please excuse me for questioning you so much," Solana apologized, "I do not intend any lack of respect, and speak merely from my great concern for Altazar. I was not happy to leave him there so unprotected."

The Mother-Moon gave him a look of loving compassion. "We understand that, my dear. There is one thing which you could do that may put your heart somewhat at rest. There is a woman who lives but one night's journey from here. She is a hermit who is known to see everything. She does not often extend her welcome to strangers, but I know that she will recognize you. She will be able to tell you about the fate of Altazar. It is a difficult journey there; the path is a secret one which few have trod to its completion. Of course, the hermit is happy to spend as much time in the privacy of her silence as possible. If she were more accessible, she would most likely be deluged with visitants with no time alone in which to scan the Akashic Chronicles."

"You shall have to wait until the Moon is in her phase of fullness, for that is the only time when the path reveals itself," explained Father-Sun. "Until then Solana, we have much that we wish to share with you here."

*　**　***　****　*　****　***　**　*

Thus it was that Solana, Priest of Rapan-Nui, did enter the hidden Kingdom of AN and receive a great welcome there. And thus did he recognize it to be his real home. He had never before experienced such peaceful fullness.

During this time many doors to the Mysteries were opened to him. He was initiated into the Temples of the Sun, the Moon, the morning star termed Chas'ka Collya, as well as the arc of the Rainbow, and Illapa—the Thunder/ Lightning one. Each temple that he entered was a further step into the awakening of his deeper knowing. Here he reached full maturity both as a man and as a God.

As time passed by, the Moon neared her fullness and Solana awaited the evening when he would begin his solitary journey to visit the hermit woman. Knowing full well of his impending arrival, I prepared myself to receive him.

CHAPTER TWENTY:
THE HERMIT OF
THE CRYSTAL MOUNTAIN

The Moon arose over the mountain peaks, illuminating everything with its bright softness. She was finally at her fullest. Thus the perfect moment had arrived for Solana to set out on his solitary quest to encounter the elusive hermit woman who saw everything.

Aka-Capac set off with Solana, leading him upwards and northeastwards from AN. The path that they followed was almost invisible; it obviously was not much used or known. They climbed onwards until they reached the summit of a high pass through the mountains. There stood a rock cairn called an *apachita-waka*. This served as a shrine to the mountains spirits or *Apu*. Aka-Capac explained all of this to Solana as he carefully placed a rock that he had brought with him from AN upon the pile as an offering.

Solana gazed down at the hidden valley far below. He could see the Pyramid of Anani rising through the night mists bathed in silvery moonlight. It was wrapped in an aura of deep mystery. Again that pang of familiarity struck him.

"I know this view well. I have seen it many times before, perhaps in some of my dreams," he told Aka-Capac, much bemused.

Aka-Capac made ready to depart for whence they had come. "The trail begins on the other side of this pass," he explained. "It is extremely subtle and cannot be seen by ordinary men. It can be perceived only by those with the inner sight. The path is delineated by white luminescent rocks which reveal themselves only when the Moon is at her fullest. Follow these stones and fear not where they shall lead you. Sometimes it may appear as if the trail steps off the side of a cliff or ends nowhere. Focus with your true sight and you shall have no problems in finding your way. When the light of the first dawning appears, you shall be at your destination...My blessings go with you, dear brother," Aka-Capac bowed ceremonially with arms upraised to Solana who returned the gesture.

"Aka-Capac, how do I find my way back to AN?" Solana asked.

"Let the hermit reveal that to you," he replied with a smile as he waved farewell and was gone.

Solana gave one final look at Anani. The clouds had almost totally obscured it yet the peak of the pyramid still emerged above the mists. "What a fantastic vision," Solana thought. "It's disappearing as if it were merely a dream."

Walking to the *apachita-waka* he placed a tiny white shell upon it. This he had carried with him all the way from Rapan-Nui. Then he continued on over the pass, all the while searching for a sign of the white stones which were to mark his trail. But he could not see them anywhere. Solana was puzzled but not discouraged. He simply sat down, wrapping himself comfortably in his magenta poncho, and began to meditate. When he felt himself to be floating within the Great Sea of Oneness, he slowly opened his eyes. Before him stretched a delicate line of shining white stones.

Thus did Solana travel throughout that long and mystical night. The path did indeed endeavour to play its tricks upon him, yet Solana was fooled not. His inner vision led him straight and true. He faltered not, nor stopped for rest until the dawning drew near. Then he spied a small pool of clearest water that was carefully outlined with shining white rocks. Carved into the nearby rock face were the words:

A GOOD PLACE FOR TRAVELERS
TO REFRESH THEMSELVES
AND AWAIT THE DAWN

A gourd dipper rested upon a seat built out of stone. Solana sat himself down and dipped the gourd into the water, sipping it slowly. The water was cool with a refreshing deliciousness. He soon felt his fatigue slip away.

In the predawn darkness nature prepared to awaken. He could feel the stirring of birds, animals, and plant life all around him. The air itself was pregnant with anticipation of the arrival of the Sun. Nature seemed to whisper, "It comes again. There *will be* another day of life and light!"

As the sky grew ever brighter and the chill of the night began to fade away, Solana continued on the final segment of his long night's journey. The path crested a hill and there the dawn broke open as the glorious Sun One emerged radiating warmth and life renewal to everything and everyone equally. *(Remember that the Sun has no favorites; he shines on all.)*

Ahead of him Solana spied a humble dwelling of stone tucked into the side of an imposing mountain. Beside it tumbled a small brook with dancing waters. There were trees of many kinds, splendid trees and flowers everywhere! The air was filled with myriad songs of birds. An elegant deer stood calmly drinking from the stream and raised its graceful head to glance at Solana with quiet curiosity.

"How extremely beautiful! What an enchanted place to live," exulted Solana. "But it is rather isolated for a woman to live here alone. This hermit must be quite an unusual person." He truly knew not what to expect. During the long duration of the night he had pictured the hermit as many different types and ages of women. He had not thought to ask in AN whether he would be meeting an old crone or a young maiden.

He could see now that the house was round and had a tower-like room on top of it which appeared to have eight sides. Approaching the door, Solana noticed a small golden bell hanging next to it. With a sense of nervous anticipation he softly rang the little bell. There was one clear note, then the sound of movement within came nearer and nearer to the door until it slowly opened.

Green eyes met green eyes. They looked into and beyond each other. Solana thought for one dizzying moment that he was looking into a mirror. "Am I looking at myself, or am I perhaps being tricked?" he wondered. Those other green eyes continued to melt into his. It was as if they were both sinking deeply into an endless pool, tumbling, swirling around and around, then finally merging into One. Solana stood as if transfixed. It was with considerable difficulty and will power that he finally separated himself and moved back into the individuality of his being.

"I'm . . . I'm So . . . . I am Solana," he stammered. For the first time in his entire life his incredible poise and balance seemed to have abandoned him.

"Soluna," said she with a smile.

"No, Solana," said he, pointing to himself for emphasis.

"I am Soluna," she repeated firmly.

"Why do you say the same that I say?" he asked. "I am Solana."

"You are not understanding. My name is Soluna," said she.

"How can you be Soluna when I am known as Solana? Are you trying to confuse me?" he asked in perplexity.

She smiled again. "It is simple. You are Solana. I am Soluna. Cannot you see our connection?" she asked. "We are twins. We come from the same star seed."

"But I have seen you not before," Solana protested. "Yet, that is not entirely the truth, for you are as familiar to me as I am to myself. But I know you not from this embodiment; how can that be?"

She laid her finger softly against his lips. "We will speak of this later. We have many things to talk about and much to rediscover. But that must wait for awhile. Come, the hermit awaits you within."

Soluna led him into the little house. The room was filled with brilliant prisms that danced and swayed to and fro. It was sparsely furnished save for numerous crystals placed in niches where they caught the light from a sky opening. Sitting on a low stool in the corner was a woman clad in white. Her entire being emanated a strong white light which seemed to brighten the entire room. Solana stared at her with intense interest but could not make out her features clearly. They appeared to be constantly changing. Appearing to be timeless, she could not be pin-pointed within any particular age. She truly gave the impression of being all women in one. Could she not shift her consciousness freely through the dimensions and move fluidly among the oceans of time and space? Thus she could know all thoughts, experience all emotions, truly see out of the eyes of anyone who had ever inhabited this planet. The hermit was rather a limitless being and quite unlike anyone Solana had ever encountered before.

The hermit's eyes gazed into the records of his soul as she spoke to him thus:

"Welcome to this hidden place. I am the one whom you seek. I am the Hermit of the Crystal Mountain. I am extremely pleased that you have managed to make it thus far, Solana. Your arrival in AN has brought tremendous joy to them. You have served well your Higher Purpose, Priest of Rapan-Nui." She gestured for Solana and Soluna to sit down.

Solana bowed with utmost respect and settled himself comfortably on the floor in front of her. Soluna seated herself by his side and he experienced the strangest feeling that he was in two bodies simultaneously, his and hers. They both listened to the hermit attentively.

"You have traveled to this remote place for two reasons. The first one, of which you are already aware, is to inquire into the fate of Altazar, High King of Arnahem, is it not?" Solana nodded his affirmation. The hermit continued, "The second reason, of which you are as yet unaware, was to meet the woman who sits beside you. She is the one who has always been beside you, but of that you did not remember until now."

"We will speak first of your friend, Altazar. Let it be known that you have done for him a great service. He is now freed of his enchantment. The woman Mu'Ra of TI-WA-KU lives upon this earth no more. She is dead by Altazar's hand, killed by the same dagger that was intended for you. She has finally been returned to her people and I shall assume that she will remain there for some time."

She continued, "Understand that Altazar is lost to all of us for the present. He enters a period wherein he will disappear from history. That does not mean that he shall cease to incarnate upon this planet, that he shall. In fact he will continue his path of service and will constantly be observing and learning. We are watching carefully over him. It was written in the scripts of his chosen destiny that he would fall, thus fall he did. But I shall state that there is a higher purpose to his chosen path."

"Now, as the Phoenix, he must begin his lengthy ascent to full remembrance and forgiveness. The one whom he must forgive is himself. It has not yet been determined when you shall encounter him again, but one day you shall. Remember, that when you do, he will have but one chance to forgive himself for the harm that he almost brought to you. If he cannot, he will, once again, be lost for untold measurement of time. If he frees himself of his guilt and consciously awakens his memory, then he will be permitted to come to the Crystal Mountain one day and know complete and perfect healing. He will therefore be fulfilling his Higher Purpose."

"You see, there are many highly advanced souls serving on earth at this time who have volunteered to undertake experiences which appear to be a state of *falling from grace.* However, intrinsic to the *falling* shall be the *rising.* When these ones arise, not only will their personal karma be transmuted, but also a large portion of the planetary karma that they carry for all of us, shall hereby be cleansed. Altazar and the others like him who have chosen to take on heavy responsibilities make an immense sacrifice for the rest of humanity. Unfortunately, since they are currently experiencing the state of *falling*—they don't remember why they have chosen their particular path. It would be incredibly easier for them if they did. Anyway, Solana, you need not worry about Altazar any more. Simply release him with unconditional love and forgiveness."

The hermit paused and stepped into the Silence for a time . . . . Finally, she spoke again:

"Solana and Soluna . . . Think you not that it is remarkable that you two bear such a resemblance? At last you have found each other. You are what is known as Twin Souls. Now that you have reconnected within this time/ space dimension, you will never know separation again, though sometimes you may be continents apart." The hermit's beautiful smile warmed the entire room like sunlight itself. "You are hereby given four days and four nights together."

"Then Solana, you must depart here for AN in order to complete the final leg of your lengthy journey to Atlantis. You will have important work to achieve there. Soluna is my apprentice and must stay with me for the present. The advanced civilization of Atlantis now doth approach its own time of completion and you are needed there, Solana. After Atlantis, you will be sent to a new land which is being prepared to receive a direct infusion of Light from the AN focus as well as some of the chosen survivors of Atlantis. Soluna will join with you there. Understand that will be the time when your Purposes unite."

"I will not meet with you again until the end of the next cycle. Farewell, my friend. This hermit has been most honored by your timely visit. Soluna will now take you to her hut within the forest. It is time for me to return to the Silence."

"My final words to you are: First there were the Stars—from that came the Angels—who became the Humans. Now it is time to reverse the process. Forget not your Golden Wings!"

Solana bowed once again with tears in his eyes. "Hermit, I thank you profoundly for sharing with me your clear Vision. I shall always look forward to that distant day when our paths shall again cross!"

The woman Soluna took the man Solana by the arm and walked with him to the doorway. Together they stepped outside into the vibrant glowing morning.

CHAPTER TWENTY-ONE:
TWIN SOULS

S oluna led the man from Rapan-Nui through the forest to her modest dwelling nestled deep within the trees. It, too, was of stone and of circular design. Inside there was very little save a sleeping mat covered by a magenta poncho similar to Solana's and a small fireplace for heat and cooking.

"Come Solana, sit down and rest yourself for awhile while I prepare us something to eat," she said with firm tenderness.

His eyes held hers with unspoken yearning. "I just want to look at you and touch you and hold you," he replied, feeling a tremor of new emotions break loose inside him. "How can I think of food? It is you, Soluna, whom I have been hungering and thirsting for all my life and I knew it not until this very day."

"It has been the same for me, Solana. I was told about you and that one day you would come to me. Now that this moment is here I am simply overwhelmed with the loving feelings that I have for you. It is as if a cavern deep within me that had been sealed up for thousands of years is finally being opened. The freshest of pure air is streaming into that sacred hidden place and I am almost dizzy by it," she explained breathlessly. "But first I am going to feed us, so you may as well sit down and be comfortable." She smiled warmly, radiating her special strong beams of clarity at him.

"Then I shall obediently sit down and try to be patient, but I promise you that my eyes shall not be able to leave your loveliness for one instant."

The woman set her attention to the task of providing nourishment, feeling his gaze ever upon her. She wondered at the marvelous floating sensation that she was experiencing.

They ate their simple meal in silence sitting side by side. When it was finished, she said to him, "Now I am going to clean the dishes in the stream. You are to lie down and get some rest until I return to you." He was about to protest, when she kissed her finger and placed it gently against his mouth. "Trust me, you need to rest. I will return to you soon."

He acquiesced, realizing that he was actually quite exhausted. He had slept not since the night before he had set out upon his journey to the hermit. Solana laid himself down on her sleeping mat, covering himself with his magenta poncho, and was quickly asleep.

When he awoke, it must have been late in the afternoon, for the shadows had lengthened outside. Next to him the woman Soluna slept soundlessly. He covered her sleeping form with his poncho and lay there marveling at her nearness. He wanted to breathe her pure essence into himself, to melt with her until indeed they knew no more separation, to unite with his sweet partner into the vast mysterious Oneness. She stirred softly and he moved closer to her and pulled her into his arms and lay there quietly holding her. He knew perfect, peaceful wholeness, not realizing until now that such a state could exist with another person. Solana kissed her gently on the forehead. Then her eyes slowly opened and she looked at him with wonder. Taking her face in his hands, Solana brought it closer to him and kissed her on her lips. In the stillness they looked into each other and drank deeply from the pool of their shared Essence.

Finally Solana murmured, "I truly love you, Soluna."

She answered him dreamily, "Yes, I know that. And I love you as well, Solana."

"Would you tell me about Twin Souls?" he asked

"Certainly, my love . . . back at the Beginning there is but the great Oneness. Then a piece of spirit is split apart and given a soul and that soul is sent forth to manifest its destiny. This soul experiences the world of form and limitation in order to evolve itself back into conscious union with that original Oneness. The word, *conscious*, is important here. Because in the Beginning when we were within that Oneness, it was the only reality which we knew. In order to know True Union *consciously*, we must first experience the illusion of separation."

"Often souls are split apart into two or more distinct beings. These fragmented beings must learn to be complete within their limitations. When that is achieved, then they are allowed to unite with those other ones who also spring from the same seed or pool of Essence."

"The hermit has told me that each of us, I am speaking here of you and me, equals two. This is because we each contain the Sun and Moon, masculine and feminine, united and balanced within ourselves. Is that not the true teaching of AN, the God who symbolizes the unification of Sun and Moon which is also the union of the two tantric polar opposites and the balancing of the Four Directions into One? In a sense you could say that AN represents that state of consciousness which lies beyond the realm of duality. Instead of focusing on the opposite halves of the circle, we concentrate on the wholeness of the circle itself."

Soluna continued, "Well, we have each achieved that level of completeness within ourselves individually. Hence we are now ready to join with one another. The hermit also says that two plus two equals the forty-four. What this represents is that when two complete-in-themselves halves come together, the sum is far greater than it would be for normal incomplete halves joining. It moves to a higher dimensional octave symbolized by the forty-four which is a Master Vibration Number. It is also the number of absolute balance of all the opposites on multilevels of expression. Forty-four's color is magenta which is why we have these ponchos. It is the most sacred number of AN as well." Soluna paused for a breath and looked at him carefully to see if he understood all this.

Solana looked at her with delighted amazement. "I do understand what you are saying; it explains much to me. But tell me, after we unite, will there still be others that our one being, the Solana/Soluna, will join with?"

"Yes, there will be. It goes on and on because everyone and everything derives from the same original source, do they not? We all contain the spark of *chi-ta* or Divine Essence that is of the Oneness. The first degree of union or mating, such as we represent, is special because we then form a unit or partnership that will be serving a joint purpose far greater than either of us could achieve alone. Once we have truly mated nothing will ever separate us again. It will only be the product or Oneness of our union that can unite with others. We will not be uniting with others so much on an individual basis, but rather with our Solana/Soluna unit. But our unit can join with other units until this entire world is completely reunited once again."

Soluna continued earnestly, "I hope that I'm not making this all sound too complicated. It's really rather simple. The hermit also reminds me that it is important for us not to get stuck into a linear way of thinking. This is because, in reality, we live within a multidimensional universe. Multiple dimensionality is never stuck within the limitations of the time/space framework that we operate within on this planet. We belong to multiple lineages, unite in myriad unknown ways all the time, and can even experience many simultaneous lifetimes within numerous parallel dimensions. So the entire scope of the true picture is far vaster than anything our limited consciousnesses can currently comprehend."

Solana let this penetrate into his inner knowing. "I see many new aspects now. It is an incredible awareness that shall definitely expand my being. I think that you have learned far more than me," he stated.

"No, that is not true, my love," Soluna replied. "We each contain levels of understanding which the other possesses not. These are the gifts which we bring to each other. You have as many things to teach me from your body of knowledge as I have to share with you. And don't forget that we have much joy and healing nourishment to share with each other as well." She looked lovingly at him, then reached for him and brought his mouth to hers.

They kissed .... a long deep loving kiss .... a kiss that flung open wide the gates of separation between them. As their lips touched, Solana saw a vision in his mind's eye of beautiful flowers of purest white, growing from newest bud to blossom to fullness.

"Solana, I have waited for you for such a long time," she cried. "There were times when I thought that I would die from the pain of my loneliness. I have dreamed of this moment above all else. Sometimes, desolate, I despaired that you would ever come into my life. There were times when I even questioned your existence. I knew not if I was foolish to be waiting for you. The normal world held no interest for me. I could not involve myself in its silly, childish games, its animal passions, the constant mindless struggles and sorrows. So I was sent here to visit the hermit and here I have remained. In these hidden mountains I have found delight in the flow of nature, the simplicity of each day, and above all, the Silence. I learned to love being alone and have finally found a quiet peace within. Never have I missed the drama of the world nor the chatter of its people. The only one whom I have yearned for is you—for you are my outer balance and completion." Her large green eyes misted with tears as she turned towards Solana.

"Soluna, woman of my heart and soul," he whispered huskily, "come to me that you may wait no more."

Thus passed the four days and four nights given to Soluna and Solana to share together. Surrendering totally to one another, they experienced that Higher Being which was their unified self. They reconnected and realigned themselves to become that Oneness. They laughed and played and danced hand-in-hand through the forest wild. They drank deeply of each other until they knew no more thirst. They felt the release of the fulfillment of their dearest desires wash away all tears and struggles and loneliness past. They had fused their bonding.

And although they lived yet in separate forms, they had been reborn as One.

CHAPTER TWENTY-TWO:
ACAMA

Altazar lay where he had fallen in the slippery mud. The incessant rain numbed his senses. The nightmares gnawed at his brain, shooting it full of twisted visions. There was Diandra in his arms soothing him with murmurs of love. Then her face contorted with immeasurable pain and disappeared from view. There was Mu'Ra caressing him while muttering her dark incantations to entrap his soul. The worst picture was of Solana, his faithful friend. Had he really sunk so low as to have almost murdered him? Altazar moaned and wept, his tears mingling with the fallen rain. He wanted to die, to end his misery of pain, loss, and endless guilt. He would never be worthy again. All he knew any more was destruction—of his life, his soul, and of even his sacred Purpose. He had failed.

Through it all the storm grew fiercer and a driving wind added its eery howl to the downpour. At this point, our noble High King laid down his life and submerged his self into sleep—the sleep of forgetfulness and letting go.

But, alas, he was not allowed to remain within that peaceful stillness of the Sea of Oblivion for very long. *(Life is not usually that merciful or easy to slip away from. Are we not called back here again and again? Is there really any true reprieve save completion?)* So Altazar, he too, was called back and waved away from the shining light at the end of the long dark tunnel. And the moment came when he could avoid himself no longer. The awareness of this dimension returned to him. The world had not chosen to release him. . . . .

First Altazar heard sounds emerging through the darkened night of his soul. They were the simple, natural noises of life—a rooster crowing, somewhere the cry of a baby followed by the muffled sounds of its mother tending it.

"Oh no, I am alive yet," thought he with despair and self-pity.

Forcing himself to open his eyes, he stared straight into the eyes of a woman who was looking at him with love and devotion. She was quite young, almost a girl really, and had an innocent face both wide and clear. Her black hair shone a dark blue as the sunlight fell upon it.

Something about him felt very different. An odd feeling swept over him as he became aware of his body. He moved his hand into his line of vision. And then he realized with a shudder of recognition what had happened. The shock caused a convulsion to rock his body, for he stared at the tiny hand of a newborn baby! Altazar's eyes screwed up as he began to cry, but his cry was not that of a man, it was the shrill note of an infant. The woman moved to comfort him and thrust her breast firmly into his mouth. This surprised him so much that he could not cry and began to drink. Altazar drank deeply of her warm milk and felt a peacefulness settle into him again as he slowly slipped back into sleep.

When he again awoke he found himself tightly wrapped in a cloth that was tied around the same woman. He felt warm and secure. They were lying in a hammock which softly rocked back and forth. Around them he recognized the chattering sounds of monkeys and the occasional calls of parrots. They must be in the jungle then, he surmised. Somewhere, not too far off, someone was singing a low chant in a language that he understood not. A wave of sadness engulfed him. He did not want to be here. He did not want to remember. Altazar began to cry once more. The woman stirred beside him and whispered some gentle words as she put him to her breast. Again he experienced the warmth and love entering him.

"Maybe this life won't be so painful. Maybe I can help these people," he thought as his small hands held to her and he sucked deeply.

Thus Altazar grew up in the jungle. He discovered that he was part of a tribal group which migrated together, hunted together, and shared with each other. He learned their language, played with his brothers and sisters, and practiced hunting skills with his father. Yet there was something within him that regarded himself as separate from the others. They were his parents, his family, his tribe; yes, that was true. But he knew deep inside that he originated from something far different—somewhere ever distant which he could almost recall. The others felt his strangeness as well and he was given the name of Acama, "The One From Far Away."

As Acama/Altazar grew to manhood he began to introduce improvements into the life of the tribe. They were methods and levels of awareness that had not been present before. At first, it was small things, like a new way of making a fishing hook that was both simpler and more efficient. Then greater things, like new methods of cultivation and tools, were gradually brought into practice. By now the people recognized Acama's special talents and wished to bring him presents to show their gratitude. These he steadfastly refused, saying that they owed nothing to him and that he owed the world far more than he could ever repay. They understood this not, but out of respect, stopped offering him gifts.

Next, the women of the tribe tried to favor him by cooking him special dishes of great delicacies. But here too, they met with no success. He thanked them, then passed on the food to those most in need. He ate little himself, contenting himself with only a bowl of the poorest gruel each day, occasionally adding to it small pieces of wild fruit or fish when it was plentiful.

When Acama had long passed the initiation rite into manhood and still did not marry, this also, began to cause much concern among the people. The young women, especially, devoted a good portion of their daily gossip to this problem. All of them were quite willing to be his chosen one. Some were even bold enough to pursue him with their best seductive wiles, but Altazar was never tempted. Finally one day in exasperation, he called his mother aside and begged her to explain to the women that he would never marry. "I know not why, but I choose to live alone this life, so please persuade the young women to set their desires elsewhere," he pleaded.

His mother understood not his reasoning, yet she knew that he was special and not to be judged by the standards of others. He was of such benefit to their people; they simply had to learn to respect another of his strange habits. And thus they did.

Altazar/Acama taught and served his tribal people faithfully, never taking anything for himself. He always lived alone owning only a ragged old hammock that someone had discarded and an undecorated loin cloth, always giving fully of himself when needed.

Many years thus passed. Then the old chief took ill. There were constant murmurings among the people for all knew that he would soon die. A successor must be chosen. A small delegation approached Altazar/Acama and implored him to become their new leader. They were shocked by his angry response, for this was the first and only time that they were to see any display of temper from him. The small group shook their heads sadly and whispered to each other of their perplexity. They understood not why this man who served them so ably would not allow them to honor him in any way. And then to become angry when they offered him the position of Chief! Why any of them would be privileged to be so fortunate! Finally since they could not have Acama himself for Chief, they chose his younger brother, thinking that, at least, he would have some of the same blood running in his veins.

Thus Altazar's life passed smoothly among his jungle tribe. He lived to a fine old age, rare among these people and he continually served them well. He was understood not, but he was accepted and respected for his gifts. He gave of himself totally, yet he felt as if he never could give enough. His long path of atonement had just begun. The pattern endlessly repeated itself throughout various cycles of reincarnated lifetimes. He lost not his overriding sense of guilt. Yet he served and served, giving freely to others, but consistently denying himself.

Oh Altazar, see you not the truth that is present here? Is it not long overdue for you to learn to serve yourself as well as others? The time has come for all of us to make an end to our denials. Those many lifetimes of service were not in vain; they served their purpose, but please, can you finally step forward into the light of self-forgiveness? Only then shall you experience true healing and completion.

CHAPTER TWENTY-THREE:
THE TOWER OF LIGHT

The morning of the fifth day dawned with a rosy exuberance. Soluna led the man, Solana, to the banks of a nearby river. The time for their parting had come. They stood quietly gazing into soft, mossy green eyes which mirrored each other.

Breaking the magic of their silence, Soluna said, "It will not be long before we are together again, my love. The hermit has told me that we will found a new lineage, another manifestation of AN in a land far across the Great Ocean which shall be known as Egypt. I shall meet with you there." She paused as she felt herself brimming over with delicate emotions.

Solana took her hands and held them tightly in his. He tried to speak . . ."I have simply no words to express what I have experienced with you. Farewells are no longer easy for me, but I know that as part of me remains here with you, part of you comes with me wherever I go." He kissed her once again. "Now, my beloved, please show me the way to return to AN."

Soluna pointed out to him the winding course of the river. "Follow this and you will find yourself there in a very short time," she explained.

"Is it that easy?" Solana was much surprised.

"Of course, the difficulty always is in the finding of a hidden place. Therein lies the testing. Once you are accepted, you need be tested no longer, hence the return is simple," she replied with a loving smile.

He took her into his arms and they kissed deeply for the final time until they should meet again far across the world. Then slowly letting her go, he said, "Until Egypt, my most precious one," and Solana turned towards the river and followed the well-marked path beside it. As he was about to disappear around a bend, he turned towards Soluna and waved gaily. She stood watching him leave with a sweet smile on her lips as she blew him a kiss on the wind.

Thus was the painlessness of their parting. They both knew that they had separated not. This filled the morning air with sweetness rather than sadness.

The journey back to AN was noteworthy only in its ease. Before much time had elapsed, Solana could hear the rising wisps of music on the wind. Then the sound of one of the long mountain horns resounded from a nearby peak announcing his impending arrival.

Solana wished that he could stay here forever. Ah, to spend the rest of his life with Soluna in AN would be perfection itself. But he well knew that his life held a higher purpose which he was bound to follow and serve above all else. So letting go his beautiful fantasy, he prepared to enter AN.

He was not surprised at all to encounter Aka-Capac waiting patiently for him. Solana felt a strong bond of kinship and trust with him. They both broke into happy laughter and embraced warmly. No words were needed. Aka-Capac just looked at him keenly and nodded with a wise grin spread across his distinguished face.

They soon entered the portals of AN, albeit different ones this time, and proceeded directly to the Pyramid of Anani. Again they climbed the steep stairs to the fourth level and entered therein. The Ancient Ones awaited them with anticipation.

After they had exchanged fond greetings, the Father-Sun spoke, "Solana, you have conducted yourself well. The hermit speaks highly of you."

Solana felt his eyebrows rise in surprise. "How were they in contact with her?" he wondered.

The Mother-of-the-Moon added, "We are extremely happy for you and Soluna. She has awaited your arrival for immeasurable years. This woman has long deserved a worthy mate; it has saddened me to see her thus deprived. AN is most proud to have you here, my son."

"You seem to know everything about me," Solana blurted with astonishment while asking himself what had happened to his famed composure.

Everyone laughed heartily at this and the air vibrated with love and openness.

"That is because we are a true soul family here," Aka-Capac explained. "What need have we for secrets from each other when we all derive from the same Essence?" He laughed deeply while throwing his long elegant arm over Solana's shoulder.

"Now Solana, we must speak of more serious matters again," Tayta-Sun interposed. "It is essential that you complete your journey to Atlantis immediately. We have pondered repeatedly the best way for you to travel there. The problem arises in the corruption which is now rampant in Atlantis. Little time remains for its existence. Dark forces are now in many positions of power. It is preferable for you to arrive there as quietly as possible, for enemies of AN and of the Light would harm you if they could."

"The easiest way for you to enter Atlantis unobserved would be for you to depart here by raft following our sacred river, *Wilka-Mayu*, until it joins with the Grandmother Lake to the north which empties into the Great Ocean that surrounds Atlantis. However, this method of travel would require too much time and Atlantis now has little time left. Hence we have decided to send you by a faster method, although it is also slightly more dangerous. We are not involved in teleportation here in AN such as is practiced in Atlantis and previously in Lemuria. Our method is a form of interdimensional travel utilizing the Tower of Light of AN."

Solana listened to all of this with a growing sense of awe. "Will I ever return to AN?" he asked as he was struck by his sadness at leaving this place of his heart.

His Mother-Moon gently replied, "The Kingdom of AN, as you have experienced it, will soon disappear from the material plane of manifestation. New offshoots of its energies will reappear in various locations around this planet. One of these you and Soluna shall begin in a place to be known as Egypt. Another will be founded near here by Aka-Capac and his sister, Coyami. You may recognize these civilizations by their worship of the Sun and Moon as equals and mates and by the fact that the founders of their dynasties are Twin Souls—brother/ sister and husband/ wife—like you and Soluna."

"The day will come when these new civilizations will also reach their time of completion. It will seem as if AN existeth not, and it will be largely forgotten from recorded history. At this point AN will remain alive only in the memories of those on earth who are still in its service. Ultimately, in the far distant future, the day will arise when those of the AN lineage remaining on this planet will complete their terms of service and be called Home to AN. Remember when that time comes, AN will no longer be found upon this planet. It shall reside within another dimensional universe which exists at a higher frequency level upon the evolutionary spiral."

The woman continued as Solana listened with rapt attention. "When you and the others are ready to return home, when you have heard its Call resonate deep within the pre-encoded patterns within your very cells, then you must focus on the belt of Orcora high above in the heavens. The center star is a doorway into our dimensional universe. Use the sounds of EL*AN*RA to take you to those three stars. Enter the spiral tunnel of the central star's luminous vortex and you will emerge through the Black Hole into what is termed a White Hole which is the stairway into the universal octave which contains a purple sky. Then if you are truly ready to return to AN you will remember the sounds I shall now give you which will draw you to us."

Leaning close to Solana, she whispered the words into his ear. Solana felt sparks of recognition electrify his body. Mother-Moon took his hand, saying "Until that day comes when you have truly completed your work here, you may remember us by tuning into the White Star which shall ever be directly overhead you no matter where you are. Stand within its radiant white and golden beams and you shall not forget us."

Solana felt the radiance of the White Star above all of them and for several moments felt as if they were standing in the midst of that wondrous orb of Light. He felt the presence there of others, many others, all quite familiar to him including his beloved Soluna. Were they not clad in long white robes and strange golden crowns, open at the top with points like rays of the Sun radiating outwards? He stood silently basking in the wholeness of his experience, having truly entered the dimensional awareness that exists beyond what is known as time and space. Then with a sudden shudder, he was returned to his physical body and realized that he was once again within the Pyramid of Anani.

"Come, let us proceed to the Tower of Light!" Father-Sun led them through the doorway and up the remaining steps to the apex of the pyramid. There they entered into a small chamber of such exquisiteness that it is nearly impossible to describe. We shall merely mention that both walls and floor were inlaid with gleaming emeralds and clear, sparkling quartz crystals outlined in gold and silver.

"There is one man whom we still trust and work with in Atlantis," the woman said in a hushed voice. "His name is Dr. Z. We are in communication with him via the magnetic grid. He is already expecting you. Much controversy surrounds him during the present time, for he has, unfortunately, acquired powerful enemies. But forget not that he is far more than he appears to be."

"What about my messages to the Brotherhood of the Seven from my people of Rapan-Nui?" Solana inquired, still carrying the weight of his yet uncompleted responsibilities.

"Much time has passed by in the outer world, my son,"

she gently explained, "more time than you are able to imagine. The Brotherhood of the Seven is now powerless and the situation in Atlantis is extremely decadent and corrupt. Dr. Z. will explain all of the details to you when you arrive there."

"Just exactly how am I going to get there?" Solana questioned.

"The process is difficult to explain with the human mind and with the limitations of words," Father-Sun replied. "But I shall try. First you must see our Pyramid of Anani as a representation of the third dimension known as the world of matter. Next visualize its corresponding pyramid, that which descends to it upside down from the sky above as the fifth dimension which we shall term the world of spirit. Understand that where the apexes of the two pyramids meet, they overlap and interlock, forming a diamond or crystal shape. This takes place in the area where we are presently standing. It represents the fusion or bridge between the dimensions of matter and spirit or form and formless. This bridge is known as the fourth dimension. This is where we are. In fact, this is one of your functions on earth, to be a fourth dimensional being linking spirit and matter."

"Now we are getting to the part that is complex to explain because first you must throw away all your concepts of spacial relationships. Know that there is no one definitive up or down; there are many. It depends merely on your dimensional point of view or reference. Visualize in your mind that you are putting the two overlapping pyramids flat on the ground and that you are sitting within the diamond where they meet." He hereby motioned to Solana to sit down on the floor within an inlaid diagram of the two pyramids. "Note that when you experience inter-dimensional spacial relationships there is no fixed point of either up or down nor of horizontal and vertical. It all depends on which dimensional viewpoint or frequency they are perceived from. Now when you sit within that diamond formed by the interconnected ascending and descending pyramids, you will see that you are sitting within a tall crystal, a transmitter of light and energy vibrations. That is the Tower of Light!"

"My dear Solana," Mother-Moon added, "in truth, numerous Towers of Light are formed from the interlocking of the ascending and descending pyramids. These are the dimensional doorways or stargates, vortexes into myriad time/space dimensions. Hence the chamber where you are presently sitting, which we refer to as the Antarion Conversion, has the capacity to send you to numerous star fields or universal frequency zones."

Father-Sun brought the conversation slightly back to earth as he continued, "When you have truly entered the diamond space in the center and the Tower of Light has revealed itself to you, then you shall be experiencing what is termed the sixth dimension. Your being shall be permeated with its penetrating Light, and you will feel the weight of your physical body slip away as the space between your molecules expands. Then you shall begin to rise upwards within that Crystal Tower of Light, (sometimes referred to as the Pillar of Light,). The journey may appear endless, for you will not be within the confines of time/space as it is commonly experienced on this plane through normal human consciousness. You will no longer be aware of yourself as a unit of individualized consciousness. You shall simply be the Light. When you finally reach what we shall term

The top, you shall find yourself in a chamber hidden within Atlantis and Dr. Z. shall await you there."

After bidding yet another sad/sweet farewell to those whom he loved dearest, Solana closed his eyes and began to concentrate upon the energies within the diamond. Soon he became aware of the Tower of Light rising high above him. It felt as if he were sitting in the center of a gigantic quartz crystal which flooded him with its Light. Slowly he felt himself lighten and begin to rise. Powerful energies beamed into him. After a while he entered a vibrant zone of pulsing redness wherein he experienced an infusion of red revitalizing his very cells. Then he was lifted into the sphere of warm orange light, more brilliant than a thousand suns, which strengthened his will. Next he rose through an area of glowing yellow which imbued his being with the light of pristine clarity and penetrating wisdom, to the emerald green which opened his heart to beat in unison with all hearts. Still Solana was lifted higher up the tall shaft of the Tower of Light, although he was no longer conscious of his individualized self. Entering the azure blue ray he heard, vibrating within the very core of his being, the Sound which contained all sounds, as he resonated in Oneness with all of Creation. Then upwards he went into the mystical indigo which held the revelation of all Mysteries. Finally Solana rose even further into the vastness of purple wherein he was truly empowered.

One color followed the next in steady succession. At last, everything became infused with a radiant magenta and all the parts of his being unified into One. That too, soon dropped away as Solana was lifted higher into the sphere which contained pure brilliant white light once again. This Light was of such magnitude that it obliterated all else.

Yet, as Solana slowly returned to the awareness of who he was, he was certain that he had now arrived in Atlantis.

Δ   *Δ*   *Δ*   *Δ*   *Δ*

Thus did our dedicated Priest of Rapan-Nui and servant of AN complete his lengthy journey to Atlantis. Soon he would be shocked beyond words to discover just how many thousands of years of worldly time had actually elapsed since he had departed his island homeland. (The explanation is quite simple, for was it not true that both AN and TI-WA-KU did indeed exist outside of time?) Yet, amazingly, Solana had not aged much outwardly, although his awareness had reached a new level of conscious maturity.

Throughout it all, he had been watched over and protected while he was carefully led from experience to experience. This we always do with those dedicated ones who never let fall their sacred duty. They glide through the difficulties of life as if on golden Wings of Light. It is not always easy for them, this we know, but if they were only aware that they are never truly forgotten by us. Most of them are just beginning to realize that they are truly the Angels who were assigned to the Earth back at the beginning of time. Such a rare and remarkable one was our devoted Solana.

CHAPTER TWENTY-FOUR:
THE FINAL DAYS

The deep, melodious tones of a man's voice broke into the Silence, "*Aztlan Antes Harone.*" Slowly the brilliance of the white Light receded. Solana could now perceive the figure of a man dressed in deep violet robes. Gesturing with fluid movements, the man was deep in concentrated prayer. Solana felt that this must be the respected Dr. Z. As he watched, the man completed his magic and raised his arms in the sign of Atlantean greeting to Solana. His keen blue eyes held a piercing intensity. They peered into Solana, subtly scanning the records of his soul. Solana spoke not, but watched the man intently, perceiving him through his own impeccable clarity. Dr. Z. emanated an aura of far reaching authority and deep wisdom. Although he appeared ageless, Solana had the impression that here was an ancient soul who had been on earth for a very long time indeed.

"Welcome to Atlantis! I am Dr. Z., but of course. And you, I shall presume, are Solana, a true Sun of AN. How are you feeling?" he asked solicitously.

Solana took a few moments to find his voice as he felt himself slowly settling back into his physical form which felt quite different than before. Answering carefully, he replied, "I am returning into the awareness of my body, but I am not completely into it yet."

"Excellent," Dr. Z. commented. "We must make haste to leave here. The Hill of the Makers is no longer a safe place to tarry. We must not be discovered. Do you think that you can walk yet?"

"I shall try to," Solana answered weakly. Dr. Z. offered him his arm and helped him to his feet. Solana stood unsteadily, leaning heavily on the tall frame of Dr. Z. "I feel a bit dizzy," Solana remarked.

"That will soon pass," Dr. Z. said kindly. "We can walk over to the wall so that you may lean against it. Here, I brought you a robe to wear. You must not walk about in the clothing of AN. There are a few here who would recognize its origin and it could prove potentially dangerous for you." Dr. Z. helped Solana pull the hooded azure robe over his head. By this time Solana felt his strength returning and could walk about unaided.

"We shall leave here by the old system of tunnels which are now unused," Dr. Z. explained. "We must step lightly and take care not to make a sound because they are always in danger of collapsing. But," he added cheerfully, "at least we shall not be seen."

Solana was led outside to a stone wall whereupon Dr. Z. delicately tapped a certain rock three times with a crystal that he had pulled out from his robes. The large stone swung inwards with scarcely a sound and they entered the darkness of the secret tunnel. Before the rock had returned into position, Solana saw Dr. Z. take an empty lantern down from a bracket on the wall. Reaching once again into the mysterious folds of his robes, he brought forth a small twinkling object which he placed inside the lantern. Instantly it burst into glowing light.

"This was a gift to me from Alorah, Highest Priestess of the Temple of Oralin," Dr. Z. explained in a hushed voice. "It is a real star and works thus when there is need of light. Alorah is one of the few in Atlantis who can be totally trusted anymore. When you meet her, notice her breastplate. It contains thirteen of these real stars. It was given to her by her starry people who reside in the cave heavens far up in the distant sky."

The lantern illuminated fully the dark, crumbly tunnels. Pieces of fallen rocks and debris littered the rough floor. Passages forked off frequently, but Dr. Z. seemed to have no hesitation as to his direction. Solana noticed how easy it would be to become hopelessly lost and confused in here. The air was heavy, but not overwhelmingly stale.

"There must be some source of fresh air still entering the tunnels," Solana thought to himself.

They walked on and on, stepping delicately and soundlessly. After what had appeared to be quite a long time, Dr. Z. motioned to Solana to stop and make not a noise. He handed him the lantern and crept cautiously forward into the darkness. After a few minutes, Dr. Z. returned. Taking the lantern, he whispered, "We give our gratitude to the Og-Min for their gift of Light." Then he blew out the lantern with one short, sharp breath. Dr. Z. held the small star in the palm of his hand where it emitted a faint glow enabling them to see dimly. They continued on until the passage abruptly ended at a wall of stone. Replacing the lantern on a wall bracket, Dr. Z. again repeated the procedure to open the large stone in front of them which barred their path.

Stepping outside once again, Solana was amazed to discover that it was now nightime. The smooth oval of silvery moon darted between wisps of clouds, casting a mood of mystery over everything. The two men pulled the hoods over their heads, hiding most of their features. They began moving purposefully downhill towards a tall spired golden gate which glittered in the moonlight.

"Do not be alarmed by anything that you see, and do not stop no matter what happens," Dr. Z. cautioned him softly.

In a few moments Solana heard raucous, wild laughter and saw out of the corner of his hood a group of naked men and women carousing on the grass. One man appeared to be pouring the contents of a pitcher of liquid over a woman who lay writhing and moaning on the ground. Bizarre beings of half-human and half-animal forms coupled with some of them. Solana felt a sickness arise in the pit of his stomach. Averting his eyes, he kept to the steady pace of Dr. Z.

Finally they arrived at the gate. Without warning, a man, clad entirely in black, stepped menacingly out of the shadows towards him. Around his neck was a heavy silver pendant depicting an eye within a pyramid. The eye glimmered a sinister dark red.

"Halt!" his rasping voice commanded. "Who dares to try to pass here?"

"You hold no authority over us," spoke Dr. Z. firmly. "Let us through!"

The guard raised what appeared to be some sort of strange type of laser weapon at them. Dr. Z. instantly pulled a ruby red crystal from his robes and pointed it at him, murmuring words which even I am forbidden to repeat. The weapon instantly dematerialized as the guard stood stunned and unable to move. Striding rapidly to the gate, Dr. Z. spoke in a voice of command—words that sounded like, "*Aztlan-Inra.*" The gate disappeared and they hurried through.

The streets of Atlantis stood ominously silent and deserted. There was a terrible atmosphere of foreboding dread permeating everything. Moving quietly and purposefully, they finally arrived at the portals of a small white temple marked only by the word, ENORA, carved into the stone above the doorway. Dr. Z. hurriedly made a high-pitched sound which caused the door to open and they rapidly slipped inside.

Waiting in the entry to greet them was a tall and slender woman with a lovely face. Her long braided black hair was liberally streaked with grey. With deep emotion, she embraced Dr. Z. firmly. Something about her bearing reminded Solana of his dear brother, Aka-Capac. Throwing back his hood, Dr. Z. introduced Solana to his daughter Namuani. Gently taking his hand, Namuani smiled graciously at him, "Welcome to Atlantis, Solana. You have traveled such an immense distance to join us here. We are truly honored to have as our guest a representative of the remarkable Kingdom of AN from so far across the world. Come, we have prepared some refreshments for you." She led them into another room where a table was spread with delicious food and drink.

Approaching footsteps could be heard and soon a large man with a shaggy white mane of hair entered the room. His presence was immense, his aura seemed to absolutely fill the room. While he smiled warmly at Solana, his eyes showed intense concentration and concern caused by shouldering what appeared to be massive responsibilites. Solana wondered if this man ever found the time to sleep.

"Solana, I would like you to meet my husband, Vanel. He is the Master Musician of Atlantis. Our temple of Enora is the Temple of Sound," Namuani explained. Vanel and Solana looked deeply at each other and found soul recognition. *(Were not Vanel and Namuani also of the lineage of AN?)* They clasped hands in friendship, then Vanel excused himself in order to return to his urgent projects.

"I apologize that my husband cannot stay and visit with you. He devotes all of his time to his work these days, searching for the Master Vibrations which will transmute the negative energies being currently experimented with in Atlantis. Right now the Makers, our caste of priests/ scientists, work night and day to create sounds of far-reaching destruction. Vanel is attempting to counteract some of these transgressions and neutralize the distorted frequencies that are used in their manipulations for increased power and control." Namuani sighed, "This is neither the best nor the easiest time that you have chosen to come to Atlantis, Solana. But apparently you are needed here now. Please try to relax while you eat and refresh yourself," she coaxed.

After they had eaten, Solana felt much more grounded than he had since arriving in Atlantis. Dr. Z. gazed at him keenly and asked, "What think you of the mighty continent of Atlantis?"

"It is far different from what I had expected," Solana admitted. " I had pictured it not in such troubled times. I guess that I expected to see the fair Atlantis that was sung of long ago on my island of Rapan-Nui when I was young.

I feel somewhat in a state of shock. Some of the things that I saw tonight, I knew not existed in this world."

Dr. Z. smiled at him with a look of warm compassion. "It was not always thus here, Solana. Unfortunately, it is now as if an awful scourge or degeneracy has possessed the magnificent soul of Atlantis. Technology now rules over Spirit. I see that the end is drawing ever closer. We have tried our utmost to prevent this. We have attempted to transmute the discord, but the best that we have managed to do is to keep things somewhat under control. There are still small pockets of light existing here, but they must keep themselves quiet and hidden because the forces of decadence now prevail."

"The Makers live upon the Hill whereupon you arrived," Namuani added. "In the olden days they led a pure existence there, dedicating themselves to their research with a true respect for the forces that they invoked. Sadly, in the present time that understanding has been lost. More and more destructive powers are being unleashed. Magic and hideous experimentation are rampant. There are innumerable power struggles for mastery and control of Atlantis. Life for most of us has become fearful and precarious."

Solana shook his head in disbelief. "But, Dr. Z., one thing that I do not understand, tonight when the guard tried to keep us from going through the golden gate, why did you not identify yourself to him? Surely, he would have let you through if he had known who you are?"

"I have many powerful enemies within Atlantis, especially among the Makers," Dr. Z. explained patiently. "There are many here who wish for my demise. Yes, I admit that I am feared by some, which does serve me as a form of protection, but it is never wise to presume upon it. I still hold control over the magnetic grid. Many would wrest that from me, if they were but given the opportunity. Without the key to the Master Grid, the forces of darkness cannot assume full power and control over Atlantis. At this point it is simply easier and safer for me to go about my business somewhat anonymously."

Solana remembered the messages that he still carried from his priests on Rapan-Nui. "What is the situation within the Brotherhood of the Seven?" he inquired, still profoundly stunned by Atlantis' impact upon him. *(Forget not, dear readers, that this sensitive soul had never before been exposed to the corruption of the world.)*

"Things have not gone well for them since the passing of their Elder many years ago. Only five of the Seven remain. They have been unable to find anyone of the quality of consciousness and dedication necessary to replace the two who are gone. This has disillusioned them immensely. This once great fraternity is now simply five powerless old men who grieve at the decay of the civilization that was once so sacred and exalted," Dr. Z. explained with great sadness and weariness.

"This is incredible, so unbelievable, and extremely tragic. For untold measurement of time I have dreamed of the moment when I would finally step forth upon the fair continent of Atlantis. Now that I have finally arrived, I am sorely grieved to find it thus," lamented Solana.

"Please Solana, do not let our situation depress you," Namuani said ever so gently. Solana could see that although Namuani appeared quiet and delicate, she had a core of tremendous courage and strength within her that was so formidable, that she need not express it outwardly.

"AN was fully aware of our troubles when they sent you here. Remember that you serve your Higher Purpose by being in Atlantis right now. I'm sure that you know that we are not always assigned to where it is easiest for us. Often we are sent to the areas of greatest difficulty for that is where the Light is most in need. Tomorrow I shall take you to meet Alorah in the Temple of Oralin. She is one of the Great Ones still upon this planet, a beautiful Angelic starry being. Now, let me show you to your sleeping chamber. You should get some rest for there is much for us to do in the morrow."

Later that night, Solana lay sleepless, assimilating his many impressions. He could no longer clearly sort out the passing of time. Was it possible that less than a day before he had been with his beloved Soluna? As he thought of her a warmth began emanating within his heart and he fell sweetly asleep.

ΔΔΔ ΔΔΔ ΔΔΔ ΔΔΔ ΔΔΔ

Thus did Solana enter into the confusion of the final days preceding the fall of Atlantis. It was difficult for him— that we knew well. But his presence was necessary for our Plan and his stay in Atlantis surely would not be a prolonged one.

CHAPTER TWENTY-FIVE:
THE TEMPLE OF ORALIN

Namuani's white hooded robe ruffled and flapped in the stiff breeze as she led Solana quickly through the ominous streets of Atlantis. They halted at last in front of a large imposing white domed temple. Above its immense portal was carved the word, ORALIN. Armed guards stood at alert attention before the massive doors. Climbing the steps rapidly, Namuani flung back her hood as she reached the top stair. The guards bowed to her in recognition and one of the doors swung open to admit her and Solana, who kept closely to her side.

Inside they were greeted by several priestesses who bowed to them respectfully while giggling and murmuring to themselves. Another one ushered them into the Great Hall. This was located inside the large domed portion of the temple. Solana gazed up at the high ceiling and noted with interest that it was painted a brilliant cobalt blue-violet sprinkled with shining gold and silver stars. Truly it appeared to be a map of the heavens, but contained far more star formations than Solana had ever before seen.

He stood transfixed looking up at the inside of the dome. Two young women came rushing into the Great Hall bubbling with excitement. Solana turned to look at them. One was strikingly beautiful and bore a strong resemblance to Namuani. Her eyes had some unusual quality to them; what was it? Solana glanced upwards again quickly and confirmed his observation. Yes, her eyes were like stars. This woman rushed to tightly embrace Namuani. The other woman had long golden hair, was slender as a reed, with an aura of remarkable depth and self-containment. Namuani beamed to the visitor from AN. "Come here, Solana; I wish to introduce you to my daughter Novasna."

Novasna turned her sparkling, starry eyes upon Solana and bowed gracefully to him. "I am honored to meet you, Sir. I would like to present to you my Temple-Sister, Avalin. She is a very close friend of my brother Anion, who is one of the Makers now," Novasna explained with great friendliness.

At the mention of her son, a cloud of concern covered Namuani's face. "How is Anion faring these days?" she inquired of Avalin.

"Not so well, I'm afraid," Avalin responded. "I am having a difficult time with him. You know how deeply we love each other, but now we spend most of our time together arguing. He, like many of the Makers, has lost all his perspective of the sacred nature of the forces which they are indiscriminately unleashing through their experiments. Increasingly, Anion craves more power and control, regardless of its consequences on the human level. He even now speaks of his own grandfather, Dr. Z., as an enemy of Atlantis who must be removed because he is hindering *progress in technology*." Avalin shook her head sadly, "I simply do not know if I can get through to him anymore. I've certainly tried."

Namuani embraced her affectionately. "I know that you have. So have I, but he barely sees me anymore. There is so much of the wild energy and brilliant genius of his father Davodd in him. Avalin, you must know that I am most grateful for your constant attempts to help him."

"I only wish that I could do more. It's as though a crazy disease has possessed many of our Makers. We will be fortunate if they don't destroy everything here," observed Avalin, who then paused and turned to Solana. "Sir, I have heard that you hail originally from Lemuria. Knew you there of a High King named Altazar?"

"Yes, I knew him well. He was my closest friend," Solana replied evenly while experiencing intense surprise at hearing Altazar's name spoken here. "After the sinking of Lemuria we traveled together from my island of Rapan-Nui to a terrible place called TI-WA-KU. It was an ancient ceremonial center near the Kingdom of AN. It was there that we were sadly parted . . . " Solana's words faltered.

"Know you then that his wife Diandra resides here in Atlantis?" Avalin asked.

"No, I knew that not," Solana said with much astonishment. "How can that be? Did she not die when Lemuria was destroyed?"

Namuani explained to him, "Diandra was forcibly teleported here at the time of the Motherland's demise by her brother Davodd, who was my son Anion's father. Davodd lost his life for that, for he did it without permission of the Brotherhood of the Seven and without full knowledge of the teleportation process."

"Oh, if only Altazar had known that Diandra survived!

It would have saved him," Solana lamented.

"She did not make the transition here unharmed," Avalin added softly. Solana could see that she cared deeply for Diandra. "Her memory did not return. She lives in this very temple but spends each day sitting silently on the shore of the Great Ocean gazing westward out to sea. She speaks no longer to people, but only to the many seabirds which flock to her. I, myself, go to her every evening and bring her back to the temple and make sure that she eats something. You see, many years ago, when as a small child I entered the Temple of Oralin, I was placed into her care. She was as a mother to me. Now, I do what I can for her."

Solana felt his heart about to burst into pieces. "If only Altazar or Diandra had known that the other was still alive, their sufferings could have been averted," he thought. He asked Avalin, "Could you possibly take me to see Diandra?"

The priestess looked at him keenly and felt his sincerity. "Yes, I shall be pleased to do so. I could accompany you right now. Alorah is in the midst of some important conferences and cannot see you until they are completed, and I'm sure that Novasna and her mother would enjoy the opportunity to visit each other, right?" The two women nodded in agreement.

Donning a purple hooded robe, Avalin took Solana with her down to the ocean. The beach was composed of finest white sand. Solana spied some exquisite shells lying about. Picking some up, he tucked them into his robe, thinking how much the sea air reminded him of his island home. They walked towards a steep cliff which loomed over a rocky point jutting sharply into the ocean. There underneath the base of the cliff, sat a solitary woman dressed in a deep purple robe. Her long hair was silver now and blew loosely about in the sea breeze. Although she was no longer young, her face was still beautiful with those magnificent eyes and cheekbones. A certain haunted vacancy of expression emanated a purity and sad innocence that touched Solana deeply.

Avalin and Solana sat down beside her on the rocky ledge. Diandra turned towards them with an air of incomprehension, then quietly returned her gaze to the sea. Avalin gestured to Solana to speak if he wished. He composed himself as best he could. "So here is the wife of Altazar whom I have heard so much about," he thought incredulously. Solana watched her keenly, trying to ascertain what degree of conscious awareness Diandra really had. A fleeting thought nudged his mind that possibly she was far more alert than she appeared. Perhaps, Diandra had simply chosen not to be bothered by the commonplaces of life anymore. But that thought quickly passed by as Solana noted her absolute lack of expression or reaction to their presence.

His voice was gentle, but tides of emotion rose and fell within him as he prepared to speak. "Greetings to you, Diandra, wife of Altazar! My name is Solana. I hail from the Lemurian island of Rapan-Nui where your husband was sent at the time of the Motherland's completion."

Diandra turned her blank expression towards him and stared without the slightest hint of recognition that his words were being understood.

Solana began again, "Your husband and I sailed forth together from my island trying to reach Atlantis." His voice almost broke down as he thought how Altazar should be here with him right now. "Altazar loved you very much.

He was filled with grief and guilt because he assumed that you had been destroyed along with his entire homeland. *(May the hermit caution all of you at this moment about the dangers of making false assumptions. Please accept the fact that we are rarely given more than a few fragments of the entire picture.)* Solana continued, "Altazar no longer wished to live, he did not want to be the sole Lemurian survivor, but he tried to fulfill his duty and journey to Atlantis as my priests on Rapan-Nui had charged him."

Solana stared deeply into Diandra's unresponding eyes trying to penetrate the veils of her awareness. Something within her had sealed itself shut. If only he could reach her. Looking at Diandra, he could see vestiges of her former magnificance. What a splendid partnership Diandra & Altazar would make. They were truly equals on every level of their beings. No wonder Altazar had been profoundly devastated! Solana felt a deep regret that Altazar had not made the journey to Atlantis. Surely he could have healed Diandra. And if he had only known that Diandra was alive in Atlantis he would not have been entrapped by Mu'Ra. Solana returned from his saddened thoughts and continued slowly.

"Due to unfortunate circumstances, I was parted from Altazar many years ago and know not of his present whereabouts. I want you to know that your husband was a true friend to me and we shared many of our private thoughts. I can only tell you, Diandra, that Altazar loved you above all others and would have gladly sacrificed his life for yours."

At last overwhelmed by his emotions, Solana could speak no more. Bowing to Diandra, he stood up to go. The woman continued to stare back at him without a word.

Avalin bowed to Diandra as well and the two of them gently departed.

Diandra sat unmoving and ever silent until they were gone. The waves pounded relentlessly upon the rocks with a steady rhythm. A few sea birds made their way back to her and perched upon her lap. The air was filled with the smell of salt and drying seaweed.

Slowly, very slowly, Diandra's lips moved as she quietly spoke the word, "Al-ta-zar." A large tear emerged from her eye and slid down her cheek. Then another appeared and yet another. She murmured over and over, "Al-ta-zar, Al-ta-zar, Al-ta-zar." The tears fell steadily, but she moved not. The tears rained down Diandra's face as a small portion of her awoke and began to remember.

CHAPTER TWENTY-SIX:
THE EVACUATION

For three days they had been silently slipping past the guards into the Temple of Oralin for their private audiences with Alorah. The High Priestess had sent out her summons with secret messengers who had combed Atlantis seeking out the chosen ones. Each individual audience did not last long, yet as the summoned ones departed the temple, a profound change could be perceived in them. There was a new seriousness of purpose as well as an aura of shock around those departing ones.

Solana sat patiently in the temple waiting for the moment of his meeting with Alorah. Finally he, too, was called forth and ushered into the smaller domed temple room where she was to receive him. This dome was composed of some sort of crystalline substance which gave it a quality of semi-transparency. Through the walls, he could faintly see the shadows of flowers and trees lightly swaying in the breeze. It was an altogether unusual effect which lent an air of supra-dimensionality to the entire room.

Alorah soon entered and approached Solana with a

radiant smile. She spoke not but merely extended her hands to him palms down over his which he quickly placed palms up. Solana felt a wave of energy surge through him. Soon he saw the Ancient Ones of AN sitting side by side watching him carefully with loving concern. He saw the hermit gazing into her crystals as she slowly fused into a crystal herself. Next he experienced Soluna sitting beside the small pool lined with white rocks where he had stopped and refreshed himself on his journey to the hermit. Soluna leaned forward to look at her reflection in the water. Instead of seeing herself, she saw Solana looking back at her at just this very moment in time. Kissing the tip of her finger, she touched the mouth of his water reflection with it. Instantly Solana felt her cool finger touch his lips. Then the scene changed and he saw a small boy living in the jungle running around with a primitive bow and arrow. He could not make out the significance of this vision nor the identity of the child.

Solana was now taken to a large cavern which seemed to be located high above in the heavens. Banks of white candles burned constantly as a low chanting filled the air with a sense of timeless peace. Hooded white robed figures walked about with graceful reverence.

"Welcome to the Halls of Og-Min," spoke a voice coming through Solana's higher mind. Even though he could not clearly perceive the faces of the others present, Solana felt that they were all well known to him, some sort of close kin. A figure stood gracefully at the heart of the cavern, a most unusual being in a body composed solely of Light! Solana had the distinct impression that this form was not a necessary part of this being, but served only to facilitate its communication with the others. It gave them something to focus on. The star being's long tapered four-fingered hands moved expressively. The name Xeron impressed itself upon Solana's consciousness. Xeron began a discourse with all those present; this was termed the Crystal Transmission. It was given not with words, but was received through crystals that each of them had implanted within their throat chakras.

Solana received much useful information during the Transmission. He saw the long covered wooden ships lying in wait in the secluded Atlantean bay. He was given his orders to go to his assigned vessel before the following evening. Solana saw clearly who had been chosen to depart and who would remain. There seemed to be nearly one hundred ships at the ready, yet part of him knew that very few of them would make it successfully to their appointed destinations. Certain Atlanteans were being evacuated, of that he was quite certain. There would inevitably be some heartrending separations, yet these orders could not be questioned or changed.

After awhile, Xeron began beaming messages of a more individual nature to Solana who had the impression that the others were also simultaneously receiving their personal instructions within this identical moment. Slowly the Halls of Og-Min began to fade away. Solana knew that they did truly exist, somewhere in a dimension beyond time, and that now the connection had been made, he would be able to return there at will. For did not part of him reside there always?

Solana looked now at Alorah, whose rare beauty could not be compared to any earthly values, and noticed her silver breastplate sparkling with real stars. Her starry eyes twinkled at him with celestial wisdom. She then handed him a sealed envelope.

"These are the secret orders for Vessel #11. Open these once you reach high sea for they shall reveal your destination and further purpose. Peace be with you Solana, Priest of Rapan-Nui and Sun of AN! Forget not the Og-Min, you are one of them as well." Alorah touched him lightly upon his forehead and was gone. Solana practically floated back to the Great Hall and sat there quietly by himself as Namuani was next summoned by Alorah.

In a short time Namuani returned in tears. Her daughter Novasna walked beside her, holding her in support. The two women cried freely and embraced each other as if for the last time. Finally Namuani signaled to Solana that she was ready to depart. Pulling their hoods up, they left the Temple of Oralin, walking rapidly and soundlessly to the Temple of Enora. Hastily mounting its white marble steps, they entered its doorway with relief.

Inside they were greeted anxiously by Vanel and Dr. Z. Namuani flung herself sobbing into Vanel's arms. He held her tightly and comforted her as best he could. "Why?" she cried, "Why Vanel? Why?"

The Master looked at her with real compassion and deep love. "You know why, Nami. Because if the slightest of chances exists that I can avert the catastrophe which threatens our Homeland, then I shall stay. Then I must stay. How can anyone measure one small human life against the possibility of saving the whole?"

"But they would not be sending us forth if we were not on the brink of an unavoidable disaster," Namuani implored passionately.

"I must stay. If I can but find the Master Sound, all negativity will be transmuted and Atlantis shall be saved," explained Vanel with an air of tragic resignation. He looked completely exhausted. The endless nights without sleep had taken their toll. Even though he was a large-boned man, he was developing a gauntness and somewhat emaciated transparency that had not been there before. "I love you, Namuani, that you well know. We have shared many full years together. Do not ask for more from me. I have been blessed with a long and full life. The small amount of it that remains, I place in the service of Atlantis. It is not much, but I must see it through. Please, dear woman, release me with your love to fulfill my final duty as you must fulfill yours." Vanel pulled her close to him and they clung to each other as they shared their tears.

During this conversation, Dr. Z. had motioned Solana aside and they stepped into an inner courtyard.

"And what are your plans, Dr. Z.?" Solana inquired respectfully, realizing that he had grown quite fond of his Atlantean friends.

"I, too, am bound to see it through to the end. I will not leave the magnetic grid unprotected. But worry not about me. I have more means at my disposal than anyone suspects." Dr. Z. flashed a hint of a smile. "I still have quite an arsenal of surprises that could be used." Dropping his voice to a low whisper, he said, "Solana, my daughter will be traveling with you on the same vessel. Please watch over her for me."

Solana assured him, "Of course I will, that goes without saying. I feel that you are all part of my larger family. I hereby pledge to protect and aid Namuani in any way that I can. I shall also hold you and Vanel in my constant prayers."

The next morning was filled with tender farewells. At last Namuani and Solana had readied themselves to depart the Temple of Enora for the final time. Dr. Z. stood silently watching his daughter and felt himself gripped with strong emotion. Vanel and Namuani said their last goodbyes, kissed their final kiss, and released each other with love to their now separate destinies. Solana and Namuani finally departed the temple and began their journey to the isolated harbor on the far side of the island which was the secret rendezvous point.

By the time that they arrived there, it was late afternoon. The ships could be seen bobbing gently in the calm waters. There were nearly one hundred of them—long, low, covered wooden boats with rows of oars protruding from each side. A crowd of people had gathered and were forming into the groups that belonged to each vessel. One person from each ship had been chosen as leader by Alorah and each of them, like Solana, carried the sealed orders as to their final destination and next level of work.

Namuani and Novasna had found each other and were saying their sweet farewells. Novasna had arrived here with Avalin. The Priestess Diandra had been left behind in Atlantis, but Avalin had arranged for her care with the temple-sisters who would remain.

Then the ships began to be quietly loaded. Lines of people patiently awaited their turn to board. Slowly, one by one, the vessels rowed out into the ocean. They rowed further and further until only small specks could be seen upon the now darkened horizon.

Thus it was that Atlantis did discharge its finest unto the four corners of the Earth before their hour of doom. Thus they rowed against time, constantly spelling each other at the oars, pausing neither for sleep nor for the contemplation of all that they had left behind. The sealed orders were duly opened and read as the covered ships moved purpose-fully towards their assigned directions. And still they rowed, knowing that there was little time, that the march of destiny waited for no one. The vessels bravely rowed on without any time or space for fear or doubts. They spread out upon the vast waters of the Great Ocean like a colony of tiny ants.

Thus it came about that the end of Atlantis did draw near. How it actually happened was through treachery. First the Master Vanel was tricked into a meeting outside the Temple of Enora by Anion and was murdered by some of the corrupted Makers. *(Anion shall tell us more of how this was done in the epilogue to our story.)*

Somehow Dr. Z. was made to relinquish the key to the magnetic grid. No one knows how or why this was done. It is a mystery as to whether he was forced to give it or gave it voluntarily to them. Some speak of him bitterly as a traitor; others search still for an explanation. But this we know for certain, Dr. Z. disappeared without a trace just before the end.

The final destruction was caused by a sound—as Vanel had foreseen and tried to prevent. When this terrible sound was created, the Great Crystal was over-charged and blew up. The thunder of a massive explosion was heard for countless thousands of miles. Thus the buildings of Atlantis began to topple. The earth shook and cracked into pieces. Gigantic waves rolled in from the Great Ocean and swallowed fair Atlantis in hungry gulps. The populace rushed here and there, utterly abandoning themselves to absolute panic. But there was no place for them that was safe. Their desperate screams were drowned out by the relentless pounding of the malevolent waves until finally there were no more cries.

Then our beautiful Atlantis heaved and turned and fragmented and sank. Save for a few volcanic peaks, Atlantis could be seen no more upon the face of the earth. The misguided Makers had finally experienced for one brief instant the total power that they had so long craved and thereby brought final destruction upon all Atlantis including themselves.

Out of the scores of covered ships sent out upon the waters, only eleven made it to their pre-ordained destinations. They were the ones fated to become the seeds of new advanced civilizations throughout the planet.

Once again, it was indeed a tragic and terrible time for planet Earth. But lest you forget and still mourn the death of fair Atlantis within your heart, please see that Atlantis liveth yet within our consciousnesses even today as you read these words. *Yes, I say unto you that Atlantis has truly risen.* The final days of Atlantis do not lie buried somewhere in the distant past. That was only to demonstrate to us the lesson. It is right now in this present age, that we are facing the ultimate test. This time, however, it entails the survival of the entire planet.

There is a particularly strong lesson in this for those who used to be among the Makers in that faraway time. Is this not the great opportunity that you have been yearning for to make amends for the harm that you created in the past? Understand that you shall not be given another opportunity like the one facing you right now. There is no more time for you to perpetrate the incorrect thought forms that caused the original downfall of Atlantis. You must find the proper balance between the intellect and the heart. Please, set aside your famed Atlantean arrogance and develop compassion, not only for humanity, but for all of the life forms upon your planet, before it is too late.

To all of you who read these words, please remember that today we are replaying the final days of Atlantis. We are given this golden opportunity to recreate the past in a more positive direction, to be the agents of healing rather than destruction, and to move the planetary consciousness fully into fourth dimensional awareness. The choice stands before each and everyone here upon planet Earth. And I ask you, which way will you choose to go?

CHAPTER TWENTY-SEVEN:
LINKED SPIRITS

Think you not that our story is complete. Have I not explained to you that it is without end? An important element to our legend must be added. Another fragment must be woven into the cloth of our understanding. By now we have learned to skip lightly across the ages, so come with me while I take you back to the days when Solana and Namuani first landed at the land called Egypt.

They settled in a place that they named Anu, (later known as Heliopolis or the City of Light.) Solana, Namuani and the other Atlantean survivors who had journeyed with them, quickly set about establishing friendly relations with the wild, unsettled tribes who roamed the region as nomads. The tribal people, although initially wary of the new arrivals, soon had their distrust turned to wonder. Surely these new people must be the latest Gods, for they had brought with them such wondrous marvels, things that they had never imagined to exist! Thus it was that with awe and reverence, these wild and barbarous peoples did easily open themselves to the guidance of the Atlantean survivors.

The Atlanteans created a vast center, the College of Anu, devoted to the teachings of the God AN—ever symbolized by the union of the Sun and Moon. They built magnificent temples and pyramids as they dispersed numerous advancements among the people. As they flourished, they were contacted by the other God-like ones who lived scattered throughout what was known as Lower Egypt. *(Some of these beings had been early Atlantean colonists, while others originated from the stars.)*

Throughout this time of immense activity, Solana continuously awaited the arrival of his Twin One, Soluna, but alas, she appeared not. With the passing of each month, pangs of loneliness penetrated deeper within his heart. Yet Solana maintained his trust that Soluna would someday arrive and continued his work with dedication.

Thus several years passed. Namuani, concerned with Solana's growing sense of dejection and puzzlement, finally persuaded him to accompany her to the Temple of Ptah in the nearby city of Memphis in order to inquire of the Great God, himself, as to the whereabouts of Soluna. Henceforth they made their journey and obtained an audience with Ptah, wherein Solana set forth his inquiry.

The Great God Ptah, *Homage to Him!*, listened patiently with his immaculate wisdom and compassionate understanding. *(Was he not one of the starry ones?)*

When Solana had finished speaking, Ptah stirred upon his golden throne and announced, "Know you not that the woman whom you seek is here among you and has been since first you arrived on these shores?"

Solana was truly bewildered by this and simply shook his head.

Ptah smiled and spoke again. "Go forth to Anu. After one moon has passed, you may return here once more. The woman who is your chosen one shall await you. There is but one requirement; the Atlantean Priestess Namuani must remain here with me. She is a necessary part of the ritual."

Namuani, although much surprised by Ptah's request, hereby agreed to stay and Solana departed for Anu more perplexed than ever before. Several peaceful days passed by in Memphis, during which Namuani was treated with much respect and hospitality in the Temple of Ptah.

On the fourth day she was summoned forth to an audience with Ptah who received her dressed in his ceremonial robes of white and red embellished with golden symbols. Wielding immense authority, he gestured with his staff for her to sit before him. Namuani noticed for the first time that Ptah's eyes were of a most unusual azure color, very large and elongated.

Focusing his powerful eyes upon her, he spoke. "Namuani, daughter of Aztlan, you have been chosen to undergo an initiation. You shall be taken to a hidden chamber deep within one of our pyramids. There you will be left alone for the passing of one night. It shall be a night that will absolutely change your life. After this experience you will understand many things that have previously been veiled to you. Fear not, for you are ready for this. Otherwise, you would not have been chosen for this process."

Holding a fiery torch, Ptah led Namuani to a tunnel which descended steeply into the earth. She felt small shivers of fear pricking her, yet she pushed them aside with her tremendous courage, for she knew well that she totally trusted Ptah. Whatever this trial entailed, she would do her utmost to see it through.

Thus they proceeded down the endless tunnel until at last, it began to rise with a steep, sloping angle upwards. They finally entered a small chamber, empty save for a sarcophagus of shining white marble. With a wave of his staff, Ptah motioned for Namuani to climb into it and lie down. That she did, feeling her heart pounding loudly with anticipation. Setting his torch into a wall holder, Ptah then passed an ankh over her body, intoning prayers and incantations in a sonorous voice which echoed throughout the empty chamber with a deep, mysterious resonance. The chanting quickly moved Namuani into her Higher Awareness. Then, picking up his torch, Ptah silently departed.

The room was in absolute darkness. Namuani lay ever so quietly, still hearing Ptah's chants repeating themselves within her mind. Then a profound silence descended upon the chamber. The woman had never before experienced such a total absence of sound. At that moment Namuani knew that she was the only being within the entire vast massiveness of the pyramid. In a sense she had never before experienced such isolation, yet, she felt not entirely alone. Other spirits were definitely here with her. She could sense their presence. Lying silently, Namuani stared up at the blackness surrounding her.

Suddenly a woman appeared before her. Then Namuani realized that it was not a woman, that it was her dear friend, Solana. She felt immensely relieved to see a familiar face. But no, her senses told her again, that is *not* Solana; that *is* a woman. Namuani stared intently at the figure in the darkness.

"Who are you?" she asked quietly, much confused.

"Hail Namuani! I am Soluna. I am the one whom Solana seeks, yet discovers not," the figure explained.

"Why appear you to me?" Namuani inquired.

"Because, Namuani, you and I are what are called Linked Spirits. You represent the part of me that is of the ancient wisdom. I represent the part of you which derives from the Angelic or starry realms," Soluna replied brightly.

"Are you and Solana not Twin Souls? I do not understand how you can be linked both to him and to me?"

Soluna smiled delightedly, lighting up the darkness around her. "There are many different forms of linkages. You and I are each unique aspects of the same spirit. Together we are able to stand with one foot in the past and one foot in the future, so to speak. We are also the link between what is termed the Earth and the Sky. My time for living within this dimension as an individual is completed. I have no more to experience here on my own. My energies cannot endure in the denser frequency patterns present since the fall of Atlantis which greatly altered both the planetary grid structure and the molecular content of the atmosphere. It is time for us to merge back together into the one spirit that we originally were. We shall combine our separate identities back into one being, one form."

Soluna continued with enthusiasm, "You see, spirits like me who originate from the pure Angelic realms of Elohim can no longer remain consciously in physical form on Earth due to the denser magnetic currents that have come into being since Atlantis' removal from the grid system. That is why the Kingdom of AN, Sanat Kumara's magnificent civilization of Shambala, the High Priestess Alorah and the Hermit of the Crystal Mountain have all removed themselves from the physical plane. In order for beings like me to continue in service here we are given linked spirits who originate from the same essence but have taken a different direction in manifestation. The only alternative way that I could stay on Earth would be to undergo a prolonged period of consciously forgetting my heavenly origin until far into the future, when my awareness would finally evolve to the point where I could remember who I was and begin the preparations to return to my starry home."

"But what about Solana, why can't you simply merge with him?" Namuani queried.

"Solana is in the same situation as I am. He too, originates from the celestial realms and has maintained that direct link within his consciousness. If we tried to unite with each other before we had merged with our linked spirits, we would be forced to leave the energy patterns of the Earth," Soluna explained with loving patience.

"I understand this not. Will Solana also need to unite with one of his linked spirits?" asked Namuani.

"Of course, only that has happened to him already, back when he was in AN as part of his initiation process there. After you and I unite, we merge into a third being. She is of a far vaster magnitude than either of us could ever be alone. Solana already is expressing his higher, combined form, although I'm not sure if he knows it consciously. That is why he is capable of achieving so much within one mere lifetime. You see, it is the two higher forms of you and me and of Solana and his linked spirit who shall unite. This is part of the process of forming the vehicle for our eventual return homeward. Do you understand this?" Soluna inquired.

"I am beginning to," answered Namuani contemplatively. She was starting to sense a deep bond of connectedness with Soluna, something which she had always felt with Solana. This was more than a feeling of sisterhood, more than even a blood kinship; it was like an alignment of Essence between them. "After you and I merge into our higher form, what shall happen to all of our individual memories?"

"They will become the personal memories of both of us. Hence if something happened to you in an embodiment 5,000 years ago, it also happened to me. *(Which is true for all of us, only we realize it not.)* We will be one being with twice the memories and knowledge. Some of our collective memory will be of simultaneous lifetimes, so occasionally it may get somewhat confusing," Soluna replied warmly. She had grown quite fond of Namuani during this conversation.

Namuani spoke with a tone of awe, "I truly knew not that such things as linked spirits existed until now. How are we going to make the rebonding between us?"

"It will take one full Moon cycle to effect the procedure. Ptah will bring you here every four nights. The transformation shall be complete ere Solana arrives to take us back to Anu with him. Here is a song for you to sing with me. It will help us through the process." Soluna began to sing in a clear, strong voice, *"Netula, Natala, Ima Botek,"* repeating the words over and over while Namuani felt herself floating out of her now sleeping form.

Together Soluna and Namuani floated up into the starry realms of the Goddess Nut, She Who Holds Up The Sky. They flew up over her great arched back and their bodies tumbled freely in the galaxies as if they themselves were stars. The heavens became a vast mirror and everywhere Namuani looked she saw herself reflected back as a star. At that moment she realized that everything was but a manifestation of herself. Every single star was her star. The entire mirrored universe contained but one glowing, White Star. *She was that sole star!* She and everything else were but the same. And that was Divine Essence! Celestial infinity twinkled and shone with the brilliant Light of pristine clarity.

This process repeated itself each night that Namuani entered the pyramid. With immense eagerness, she awaited the arrival of Soluna once Ptah had left her alone in the all-pervading darkness. Their song would begin again, *"Netula, Natala, Ima Botek,"* and they would arise once more and merge into that one star, entering the multifaceted, mirrored, starry universe that in truth, contained but one star.

With each experience Namuani could feel herself blending with Soluna as they slowly formed a new self that was far more than either of them separately.

The weeks rapidly passed by until the morning came when the initiation was complete. Entering the pyramid's chamber with his torch, Ptah passed his ankh and then his staff over the woman's slumbering form while intoning, "Arise daughter, tis the morning of your emergence!"

The woman awoke and opened her eyes with wondrous surprise. She was no longer Namuani nor Soluna, although she bore a resemblence to both of them. This reborn woman saw with a fresh clarity and heightened wisdom. Arising with graceful ease, she followed Ptah out of the pyramid into the dawn of a new morning.

Inside the temple Solana waited anxiously for the woman whom he had been prepared to meet. At the appointed hour, Ptah entered with a radiantly beautiful woman who emanated familiarity within her essence, yet there was some new unknown quality to her. Solana was struck speechless by her presence. As she approached him with an aura of glowing authority and loving grace, he bowed ceremonially. The woman smiled a brilliant smile at him with absolute recognition and returned his bow. Together they both experienced a sudden shyness tinged with a blush of growing excitement.

Solana broke the long, pregnant silence, in a voice brimming full of loving emotions, "Soluna? Namuani? No, please excuse me, for I know that you are neither of them, yet you are such a magnificent blend of both the women whom I have loved dearest. My beloved one, I have seen you before in my dreams. You are the other wing of my being." Solana fell silent as he stared deeply into the woman's clear green eyes with absolute delight and a smile, more radiant than a thousand suns broke out upon his handsome face. As he held out his hand to her, the woman brought it to her lips and lightly brushed his fingers with a kiss.

Ptah now stepped forward and stood before them in his full empowered majesty. Together, their combined Presences caused a radiant shaft of Golden Light to descend through the roof of the Temple and hold them in its powerful beam. They were embraced and transfixed by pulsations of Golden Light which irradiated them down to the core of Essence. Time stopped as they merged into the Golden Beam.

At last, the Pillar of Light began to softly disperse. The three of them had been purified anew. Ptah raised his staff and intoned, "You have hereby been consecrated as Solar Regents of the Great Central Sun. Your union has been blessed from On High. Now go forth and illuminate the illusions of duality and separation with the Light of Oneness."

The man and woman gave each other a penetrating look conveying their deepest alignment and love. Each of them still vibrated with fiery pulsations of Golden Light. Bowing deeply to the Great God Ptah, they tenderly took the other's arm and departed the temple hand in hand.

Δ   ΔΔΔ   Δ

Thus it was that Solana and his Twin Soul did finally encounter each other and serve their Higher Purpose together in the land called Egypt.

As they come together only at the beginnings and endings of major cycles, this also marks the last time they have been together until the present age. At this very moment, as you read these words, they are being drawn back together again for the final completion.

And thus it was that our dear Namuani and Soluna did happily combine their essences and now serve upon this planet as One.

CHAPTER TWENTY-EIGHT:
THE AWAKENING

The man stood alone, quietly surveying the hot, dusty landscape. He had been traveling on his own for some time. He could barely remember all the places he had visited during the past six months. One thing which he knew for certain was that this quest must be undertaken and it must be completed. After all the endless miles, he still didn't have the answers which he so relentlessly sought. Yet, he felt his entire being flooded by the overwhelming force of the memories of what he had experienced.

First he had gone to Peru, traveling to Cuzco and Machu Picchu where he felt some distant memory stir deep within him. Next he had journeyed on to Iquitos and later to Puerto Maldonado deep within the jungle searching among the tribespeople, for what? Possibly a familiar face, maybe an elusive memory, yet although he felt at ease in the humid overabundance of the jungle, something continued to elude his understanding.

Boarding a train to Lake Titicaca, he sat pensively lost within his thoughts amidst the profusion of passengers who jostled about him. At Puno, he gazed at the shimmering blue waters of Lake Titicaca and felt a deep sadness stir within him. Later that night, he paced restlessly on its shores, while the red woven poncho he had recently purchased in Cuzco's marketplace, billowed about him in the rising wind.

Soon our traveler felt himself irresistibly drawn to visit the ruins of Tihuanacu in Bolivia near the southern end of the lake. After a lengthy ride in a rented taxi, he was deposited at the archeological site in early afternoon. Climbing out of the small car, he felt himself suddenly gripped with a pervading sense of dread. He almost jumped back into the car, but knew that he must go on. Slowly, cautiously, he allowed himself to be pulled magnetically into the ruins of the temple complex.

"Such devasting memories abound here, and so little of this place has survived the ravages of time and mankind," mused the stranger as he awoke and began to remember. Walking carefully with measured stride, he approached the famous Gateway to the Sun. It was here, when he saw the Sun figure who held twin sceptres in both of his four-fingered hands, that Altazar broke down and silently wept.

After awhile he felt a small tug at the hem of his poncho. Looking down with surprise he noticed a skinny little girl with ragged braids who was gazing up at him with enormous black eyes of remarkable intelligence and depth.

"Señor, what is the matter?" she asked him in simple Spanish. "You must not be sad. Tihuanacu has completed its work here. They have all gone back home." Here she paused and gestured skyward. "We are happy for them, for they are our forefathers. My great-grandmother tells me that someday we shall join them." A cheerful smile brightened her smudged little face as she tugged once more on his poncho. "I know that you cry for my people, maybe they are your ancesters as well. But don't be sad anymore, because they are gone and they are happy in their sky-homes. Besides, today is a beautiful day, our Father-Sun shines brightly for us, and Señor, we are alive!"

Altazar gently took the girl's small hand and walked with her to one of the low temple walls and sat down. He smiled at her gratefully while wiping away the last of his tears.

"Although my memories of this place are not entirely happy ones, I am shocked to find Tihuanacu so devasted, so torn apart," he explained to her. "It was once so magnificent."

"But Señor, we tore it down ourselves. We used many of the smaller stones to build our houses and churches. It was not wrong; they were very useful building materials for us, and besides, now Tihuanacu's secrets shall remain hidden forever, except for those who already know."

Altazar gazed deeply into her large dark eyes and felt a glimmer of hope and understanding stir within his troubled heart.

Suddenly from across the temple complex, a boy shouted at her in rapid Aymara dialect. The little girl jumped up saying, "That is my brother, he tells me that I must go now. I'm supposed to be selling artifacts to the tourists. Here, Señor, is a present for you, so you shall remember."

She pressed a small object into his hands, tightly closing his fingers over it.

"Wait, please tell me your name before you go," Altazar asked, extremely touched by her gesture.

"It is Murita, which means little Mura. Adios, Señor!" she called merrily as she ran quickly away.

Slowly Altazar opened his hand and there resting in his palm was a little llama carved of a smooth, white stone. Incised into it was a small Sun above a crescent Moon.

ΔΔΔ

Some weeks later, his ship landed at Easter Island. Standing on the open deck, Altazar caught sight of the huge stone guardians and felt himself about to burst forth into song. He longed to raise his arms high and sing out a greeting in some long forgotten tongue. But as he became aware of the other passengers milling about, he contained himself and pulled his excitement inside.

Exploring this fascinating island over the next few days, Altazar experienced a sense of astounding familiarity especially when he visited the cliffs over-looking the small harbor of Orongo. He could almost see the fragile reed boat which had once bobbed so freshly in its waters. "And where on earth is my friend Solana now?" he wondered. Would he ever encounter him in order to make amends?

ΔΔΔ

And onward continued his solitary quest. Upon arriving at his final destination of Australia, Altazar made straight for the north to the area now called Arnhem Land. Keeping to himself and speaking to few people, he set out to explore as much of the territory as he could. Much of it did not fit in with his revived memories. The land itself must have undergone some tremendous changes.

Only when he ventured into the eastern rain forests did he begin to perceive how it had been long ago. Altazar hiked extensively in these mysterious, misty mountains never fearing the dreaded black snakes or other wild creatures. Somehow he knew that they posed no threat to him. He began to sense what it was to be Altazar. Here, alone in the tropical forests, he felt enough at peace to begin to allow himself the true, open expression of his being. This felt so wonderful that he marvelled at the fullness and freedom of it all. Yet, he reminded himself that it was far easier to feel thus as long as he was away from other people, nestled in the warm nurturing of nature.

The journey led next to the town called Alice Springs where he found himself a simple room in a run-down bed and breakfast. From here Altazar made a pilgrimage to Ayers Rock. Climbing the smooth redness of the monolith's undulating form jolted the rest of his memory awake and Altazar cried once more.

That night back in his small room, he sat composing a letter to his wife, Diandra, whom he had left at home far across the ocean. He knew not what to say. His heart ached for her, as it had ached for her all along, but what right did he have to be with her anymore? She had found herself, she was fully Diandra, she had claimed her power.

Flashes of scenes of their experiences together danced across his mind. They had met but four years ago, although it seemed like much longer. Yes, there had been a certain attraction between them apparent from their first encounter. Nevertheless, it had taken them awhile before they had started to remember just what their real connection was. They had married by then, when the memories began flooding in. Diandra had certainly blossomed, becoming more beautiful each day. Their house filled up with rare parrots and vases of peacock feathers. And there were moments, times when they became more than just two present day people, when they touched upon hints of the splendour of their lineages. That was when they truly united, with the love and wisdom developed within them long ago brought forth into the present. Those exhaulted moments were pure grace and kept them together in spite of the petty personal difficulties found in everyday life.

But trouble intruded into their relationship as a result of their taste together of the trueness of their beings. Diandra was able to open up and progress rapidly. She hungered to emerge as the real Diandra. Nothing else held such importance to her. And as she grew and evolved she looked towards her mate, knowing that he was her true equal, and longing for him to become that.

Here Altazar found difficulties. Yes, he knew who he was; he had no doubts as to that. Yet, he wasn't sure if he really wanted to come out and fully be himself. Remember, that the last time that he had truly been Altazar and emanated his vast inborn authority, terrible things had happened. Events that he still had not forgiven himself for. Hence, he retreated often into a stance of stubborn rebelliousness, closing off that part of his being, denying who he was.

Finally their life together had reached a state of impasse. Diandra stated that she wanted to live with Altazar, not with some shell of her beloved. The occasional glimpses of the real Altazar were not enough to build a marriage on. He felt himself torn apart in inner turmoil, not wanting to lose Diandra, whom he loved as his lifeline, his thread to the infinite—yet, still afraid to emerge. But in his heart, he knew that she was right, that if their marriage was to survive, that he could be nothing less than his true self.

Confused and torn apart, Altazar proposed going on this trip, feeling that the time apart and the time alone would be beneficial to both of them. It should clarify many things. When she took him to the airport they were aware that maybe they would never see each other again. She cried and held him close. He felt like crying, but held it inside, while saying goodbye to the most precious person in his life.

Well, the journey had fulfilled its purpose. He had reawakened. He had revisited the scenes of his greatest unreleased pains and guilt. Much of it had been let go. And now he knew who he was in the fullness of knowing. But the question remained, could he be that? Could he reveal himself not only to Diandra, but to others as well? Wasn't it easier to just try and forget, to pretend that none of this had ever happened? It would be so simple to disappear into the vastness of Australia.

Δ   *Δ*   *Δ*

A brilliant sunset seared dazzlingly across the sky outside his window while Altazar sat lost in thought awaiting the resolution of his destiny. All was silent save for the relentless mechanical ticking of his alarm clock, a steady reminder of the persistent intrusion of the passing of time.

Slowly the sunset faded into a muted memory of its former glory. Darkness descended upon the room. The clock ticked on with precision while nothing else moved save the quiet breathing of a man alone in the moonlight, awash in the sea of decision.

It was nearly midnight when the small desk light was turned on. Altazar picked up his pen and began to write.

. . . .

EPILOGUE

EPILOGUE:
A NOTE FROM THE HERMIT

Our story draws ever nearer to its point of completion—at least for now. But what is this? My ears are ringing with your questions. "What became of him, what became of her?" you persistantly ask. It is not my intention to keep secrets from you. This hermit seeks the release that will come when this story is finally complete. Then perhaps I may relinquish my role as Witness and finish my term of service to this planet Earth.

In the telling of *"THE LEGEND OF ALTAZAR"* we have touched upon the experiences of a few of the other magnificent beings who were present then as well. Now you are curious as to what has befallen them since those long ago times. I shall try to set the record straight, to satisfy your curiosity, to reveal as much as I can in the brief time that has been given to me to share with you. Hence I shall endeavour to lightly touch upon the many characters who passed through the pages of this strange chronicle and bring their histories forward.

Please bear in your awareness that this is but a fragment of the true story. Would that I be given the time to tell you of the others yet unmentioned and the myriad tales of days long forgotten. That task would indeed be endless. The true story has no end. But maybe you can discover these stories yourself, for indeed, is not one of the purposes of our legend to reawaken the dormant memories which lie hidden within you? Adding your remembrances to this small story leads to the complete history which existeth not in words within this present age. Know you the vastness of this?

Hopefully, you have developed an understanding of the principle of Duration. Of that which comes and goes, fills and empties, and of that which endures. Of the illusion of rising and falling amidst the constant all-pervading Silence. If you desire examples, simply look heavenward at the Sun, Moon, and Stars. Look to Nature for the cyclic passing of her seasons. Know you that cycles are spirals. With each completion to the place of the beginning we are always on a higher step of the evolutionary ladder.

Spirals are also found within the internal structure of crystals. Thus it should be no surprise to discover that crystals are the containers of knowledge and the true history of life upon this planet. They are the star seeds which hold the pre-encoded patterns of the wisdom of that which is *beyond* this life here on Earth, of the numerous dimensions we have yet to consciously explore. Crystals are also our instruments for transmitting and receiving, and you are hereby invited to open yourselves to them that they may reveal their secrets to you. Ultimately however, the time will come when we will be called upon to lay aside our outward tools and become the crystals ourselves.

Many of the souls whom you have encountered within these pages as well as many of the others yet unspoken, are within that sacred process of becoming the crystal. For the next level of planetary service it is essential to develop your crystal/diamond/light body. These are in the process of being formed. Are not your very molecules being transformed daily by the heightened energy patterns of these accelerated times?

Yes, the crystal tipped arrows are being readied for our bows of true action. Know you not that each of you borne upon the Earth carries a bow and quiver filled with arrows? Each day of your life you shoot off various arrows. With these you determine the direction and level of your actions, attitudes, thoughts, emotions, and even who and what you choose to share your energy with. It can truly be stated that with these arrows you create your future!

Certain highly evolved ones, almost all of whom have incarnated here voluntarily on a path of loving service, carry an additional quiver of arrows. These have crystal arrowheads and could be termed the Arrows of Completion. These represent the true mission or Higher Purpose that they have been charged to fulfill while embodied upon this planet. These special crystal arrows *must* be discharged in order to affect full completion and the subsequent liberation from this plane.

After these shafts of Light are sent forth into the world of men, *(the third dimensional sphere of matter)*, our freedom and release from this lengthy cycle of duties upon the Earth shall be achieved. Many are those who have served here since the beginning of time who will soon be released from this planet. These ones are being prepared right now for their homeward journey. Long have they endured homesickness, weariness, discouragment, and acute loneliness. Yet long have they served and not let fall their sacred purpose. Though most of them came here as volunteer spirits, it has not been easy for them living out countless lifetimes in the denser energy frequencies of the Earth. They have suffered much and sacrificed much. Now the Call to Homecoming has sounded. The final completion of their worldly destinies unfolds.

I honor these brave and steadfast souls in dedicating these words to them. Now I shall share with you more of their stories.

Δ ΔΔ Δ ΔΔ Δ ΔΔ Δ
Aka-Capac
- *a.k.a. The Man Who Walks In The Dawn*

This ancient soul has been on the Earth since the first colonization from the Sun-Arion System. He appeared in early Lemuria as Tana *(see Temple of the Dawn)*, and in ancient China as the Immortal Tan Na. He is a Sun of AN and was deeply involved with the founding of the Inca civilization in Peru. This was of a considerably longer duration than modern history acknowledges. Aka-Capac and Namuani spent several lifetimes together there. In fact, their connection dates back to Sun-Arion when they entered this planet together.

In the present incarnation Aka-Capac has been born as the son of a Turkish General. On the Summer Solstice of 1968, *Inti Raymi*, he made contact with Namuani in London. The purpose of this was to reawaken her. That was accomplished, although the rapid acceleration that she experienced was difficult for her to assimilate at the time. *(This is not an uncommon pattern. We often assign one of our conscious servers on Earth to act as a catalyst of accelerated growth and reawakening to the ones whom they have been closely connected to in the past.)*

Aka-Capac's present whereabouts must remain unknown. Possibly this small story shall seek to draw him forward or perhaps he shall choose to remain hidden. That is entirely his decision. It is assumed however, that due to the length of his planetary service and his high level of attainment, barring any unforeseen difficulties, this magnificent and noble spirit shall be free to achieve completion and return to the sphere of SIAN.

Δ ΔΔ Δ ΔΔ Δ ΔΔ Δ
Alorah
Together with her partner, the one known as Lor, they are the founders of what is referred to as the Lorian Lineage. Alorah originated not from this planet and although she appeared in human form, it cannot be truly said that she ever fully entered into human embodiment as we understand it.

Atlantis was her permanent assignment and she served there from its origin to its completion. She was the founder of the Temple of Creative Healing Wisdom, or Oralin, one of the most influencial temples throughout the long history of Atlantis. Her initiates were numerous. Among them within our story are Avalin, Diandra, Namuani, Novasna, and Soluna at various periods in history. Many of her priestesses are still at work among us today, but not all of them retain conscious memories of her. Nevertheless, she maintains a strong influence and telepathic communication with them.

Alorah sits upon the Interplanetary Commission and oversees the affairs of the feminine energy within this solar system in particular. She is especially concerned with purifying and realigning the Goddess energy which has been distorted by its prolonged immersion into the denser vibrational patterning of the dark ages from which mankind is currently emerging. In order for this change to take effect, there must be a rebalancing between the masculine and feminine so they both can claim their empowerment in order to finally unite as equals. Only when the God and Goddess can stand side by side will the Goddess energy experience the long sought after fullness of union.

It is extremely unlikely that Alorah will ever choose to return here in a physical embodiment since any influence that she feels to be beneficial to the Earth's evolution can be activated through her priestesses incarnate who carry on her work and teachings. As her initiates realize their completion and release from the Earth plane, the spiral shall turn and Alorah, herself, will be freed from her current responsibilities and move onwards.

Δ ΔΔ Δ ΔΔ Δ ΔΔ Δ

Altazar

Oh dear, beloved Altazar, if only you realized how deeply you are loved! Our High King is an ancient soul who originates from the star system of Aldebaron.

After his lifetime in the South American jungle as Acama, Altazar seemed to find a succesful mode for his incarnations in which he could serve without having to involve himself emotionally. Thus he was able to pass through numerous embodiments without burdening himself with the encumbrance of remembrance. A typical lifetime found him as a high-born prince in India who quickly gave up his worldly treasures in order to pursue the path of a *sadhu* or wandering holy man, releasing all his personal attachments as manifestations of *Maya* or illusion. On the path of detachment he need not face himself, for was he not the void? Novasna lived as his sister then and served as his sole touchstone with his emotions. Although he loved her dearly, he finally separated himself from her as well.

Another noteworthy incarnation was as a royal Assyrian, *(poor Altazar was continually born into positions of leadership, which he constantly sought to avoid.)* Although he was the youngest brother of the ruling family, in due course all of his older brothers expired due to either poor health or war injuries. Ultimately, it could not be prevented, Altazar had to assume the position of rulership. But it shouldn't come as a surprise to you, that he immediately allowed himself to be sacrificed in battle.

Altazar lives among us today and had, once again, assumed for many years what he had thought to be a serviceble disguise. However, as fate would have it, he has been recognized by many of the characters within our story. Thus he stands revealed. He has but one choice before him and that is to reclaim his power and authority.

If our beloved High King is willing to step forward and forgive himself, and to let go of his guilt, he will understand that none of his lifetimes' experiences were in vain. In truth he *fell* not. His long passage through the oblivion of forgetfullness and pain had a purpose. As he shall rise again, so shall the Phoenix, as a portion of humanity will rise with him. Thus he shall finally act as the savior of his Lemurian people of long ago, leading them to healing, completion, and freedom.

Δ ΔΔ Δ ΔΔ Δ ΔΔ Δ

Anion

The son of Namuani and Davodd grew up in the Temple of Sound, (ENORA), in Atlantis and was familiar with the creation of music from the slabs of man-made crystal. Hence, when he became a Maker, Anion specialized in the fabricating of this glassy, crystalline substance. Initially he created instruments for music as well as delightful figures of boats, fish and animals. However, although Anion was brilliant, sensitive, and innocent, he soon was influenced by some of the more negative individuals among the misguided Makers. Utilizing a combination of threats and flattery, they turned his creative artistry to making implements of magic and destruction.

Following the evacuation of key individuals from Atlantis in the covered ships, Anion was persuaded by his corrupted friends to arrange a meeting between them and the Master Vanel. They told Anion that its purpose was to discuss peace, but their true intent was, alas, one of treachery. They knew well that Vanel trusted Anion and would thereby leave the sanctuary of his temple. At the meeting a preplanned argument broke out and Vanel was shamelessly attacked and brutally murdered. The horrified Anion valiently tried to save the Master, but the forces aligned against them were too great.

This terrible act did serve to awaken Anion to the evil ways of the Makers and he fled to the Temple of Enora. There he pledged himself in alliance with Dr. Z. In the short time remaining he attempted to use his musical experience to continue on with Vanel's work with sound. Alas, this was not successful, for many of the secrets of Vanel's work had been shared with no one.

Then the day came when Dr. Z. himself disappeared—without a farewell—without a clue. Anion, in abject despair and rising panic, tried to build himself a small boat in which to escape. Then time for Atlantis simply ran out.

Anion returned to Earth once again when the Priestess Avalin caused him to be born as her son in the land of the Druids. He was an embodiment of the spirit of the Ash Tree, *Nion*, part of the secret Druidic Alphabet of the Trees. There high atop the mountains and in other secluded places he built the circular stone temples. He hath told me how this was wrought, but that is for another story.

There was another lifetime in ancient China as a hermit among the Immortals. Anion is an old soul who spends very few incarnations upon the Earth. The lengthy intervals between his embodiments are spent in the peaceful privacy of his own small, inverted planet.

Among us today as a child, this sensitive and gentle spirit remembers everything. He is being faced, once again, with the choice between negativity and Light. First, he must make the choice within himself, then he can begin to embody the wisdom that the strongest power is always the power of Love.

Δ ΔΔ Δ ΔΔ Δ ΔΔ Δ

Avalin

She is another extremely ancient one who carries with her a combination of fairy lineage with that of the shaman. In Atlantis Avalin joined the Temple of Oralin as a young girl where she was placed under the tutelage of Diandra. When Diandra was teleported back to Atlantis, Avalin willingly took on the responsibility for her care.

Sent forth from Atlantis by covered ship to the coast of Cornwall in Great Britain, she became a high priestess for the Druids, serving as a conscious link between man and nature. Avalin gave birth to two children, both of whom she drew to her womb through her vast magical powers. One was Anion who became a Druid priest and raised the stone monoliths; the other was Diandra.

Avalin has spent numerous lifetimes upon this planet. An important one that we shall mention was as a powerful priest of the Mayan civilization in the region of Mexico now known as the Yucatan. She has also walked among both the Tarahumaras and Apache Indians in North America serving as a medicine woman or shaman.

Currently living quietly among us, Avalin shall depart the planet when she is satisfied that she has been here long enough and turns her gaze from the Earth to the Stars.

Δ ΔΔ Δ ΔΔ Δ ΔΔ Δ

Bog-Lor

One lesson that he learned from his dramatic final Lemurian experience is not to demand a position of authority. Still retaining much personal power and spiritual knowledge, Bog-Lor is sought out by others because of it.

He tends to surround himself with persons of lesser evolvement so that he may hold the greater spiritual authority without a challenge. It may be noted here that Bog-Lor needs to learn to work with others who are his equals. Bog-Lor does not impose his teachings on his followers. He often lets his inferiors, so to speak, run his ceremonies, although he is the more capable. This lowers their impact, although he perceives this as a symbol that he is egoless. In this lifetime, Bog-Lor is a Native American medicine man.

Other embodiments of his have been spent in Tibet, Peru, and India gathering vast stores of personal power and ancient knowledge. Another fascinating lifetime was lived as a powerful prostitute of the Dragon Lady type in the Orient. This was one of his most difficult lifetimes and had a profound effect on his later relations with women, including coming to terms with the feminine side of himself. This is one of the major adjustments which he is currently called to make within himself.

There are other important lessons which are crucial to his further evolution which he is presently facing, *(or running from, as the case may be).* Since his power derives exclusively from the ancient energies, Bog-Lor must learn to open himself to the newer multi dimensional vibrations now entering Earth's forcefield. In order to step through the door which stands open before him, he must be willing to release all of the old energy forms that he has heretofore utilized to amass his immense body of knowledge. This he is afraid to do, fearing that he will lose his personal power in the process. *(There is a lesson within this for all of us. The time that is upon us calls for the absolute dropping away of many of the old patterns and tools which have served us nobly in the past, for now in this new dawn they shall merely hinder us from going forward with openness, clarity and grace.)*

Secondly, the magical and magnetic Bog-Lor must learn to open his heart and develop compassion. This too, is connected with his fears, mainly those of rejection and of not being loved. He surrounds himself with an aura of arrogance and quiet superiority which he believes serves him as a protection against emotional hurts and disturbances.

My heart goes out to you Bog-Lor, with your stubborn hard head and your closed heart, and such a loving being inside. You really don't fool us at all. We love you and respect you and fully understand the immense burden of what you have willingly taken on to transmute for all of humanity. We support you as you plumb the depths of the darkness of your tormented soul, calling you to return to us joyously that we may all sing with the Angels, soar through the heavens, and that you may personally find the unconditional love and release that you have long sought.

Δ ΔΔ Δ ΔΔ Δ ΔΔ Δ
Davodd

The wild and passionate Davodd is among us today, but remains much the same as he was during the time of Atlantis. His brilliant genius has finally returned but he has still not learned the proper control and focus of his energies.

I shall tell you that Davodd has encountered Diandra numerous times, as he once so fervently desired, and even briefly married her in this present age. They maintain a strong psychic connection to this day, although they rarely encounter each other. He is still immensely pulled to her, but because he cannot handle the powerful energies involved and deal with his own memories and internal imbalances, he withdraws from her. Possibly it could be noted that she fulfills the function of holding a mirror for him and Davodd is still not willing to look at his reflection. Presently, Davodd has been placed in a life situation which is forcing him to develop the much needed qualities of stability and constancy. There is hope that he shall manage to make the major breakthroughs required in this incarnation.

Δ ΔΔ Δ ΔΔ Δ ΔΔ Δ

Diandra

The beautiful Diandra derives from the Goddess Lineage. She was assigned to Earth as one of the early colonizers from the ArcAdion System referred by you as Arcturus. The original and complete Diandra was the founder of the Temple of the Forbidden Wisdom or Temple of Diandra, in early Lemuria. Hence it should be no surprise that during her final Atlantean incarnation she was, once again, sent to Lemuria.

After her traumatic Atlantean experience, Diandra was born as a Druid to Avalin. This lifetime was spent working mainly with the animal kingdom in a healing capacity.

Diandra appeared in UR of the mighty Chaldean Empire, high born and retaining many of her Goddess aspects. Here she worked closely with others from the ArcAdion System, (Akkadia). Unfortunately a basic mistrust of people remained with her as a result of Atlantis. This manifested itself as a coldness towards others and a manipulation of those whom she ruled. When she was given power and control, she tended to misuse it. *(This was a result of the fact that she had still not totally healed within her auric body.)* Thus has the Goddess energy been distorted on Earth for many an age.

Diandra and Altazar have repeatedly encountered each other throughout the course of history. Each time that they have met, they have not been ready to acknowledge either themselves or each other. Today it is essential that their conscious recognition and healing take place.

Having made great progress within herself, Diandra now knows fully who she is. Her Atlantean and Lemurian memories and wisdom have reawakened. Her special gift to humanity lies in the field of healing. First she must heal herself and fuse the link between Diandra the human and Diandra the Star Goddess. She also needs to turn her attention from animals to people. This she is in the process of doing and presently serves her Higher Purpose in work healing the emotional bodies of children and their families.

Diandra's largest lesson has been to open her heart in total loving compassion, forgiveness and trust. She must purge herself completely and let go of all the pain and anger she has stored up inside. Then she shall return to her natural state of grace and innocence. As she heals herself, thus shall the Goddess energy be transmuted and purified.

The glorious Diandra emerges once again to trace those final footprints on the long road to her completion.

△ △△ △ △△ △ △△

Dr. Z.

Ah, Dr. Z., what an enigma! After Vanel's demise in Atlantis, Anion joined forces with him and tried to continue Vanel's work. Then Dr. Z. disappeared with great mystery shortly before the Great Crystal was shattered to bring on Atlantis' fall. No one has ever known for certain what happened to him.

Throughout the long ages since then, whenever conscious Atlanteans encounter each other in various incarnations, the conversation invariably turns to the subject of Dr. Z. The questions are endlessly repeated. "Where is he? What happened to him? Have you seen Dr. Z.? Did he serve us as a traitor or as a hero in Atlantis?"

There has been vast speculation as to how the Makers ever wrestled control of the magnetic grid from him. Was he killed by them or did he flee Atlantis on his own when its destruction appeared imminent? If he had remained, could he have averted the catastrophe?

No one has ever admitted to knowing his whereabouts. Yet, the rumors have abounded—some fantastic, some plausible. Was he not an alchemist in Romania or a high priest in Egypt? Maybe he had a retreat high up in the Himalayas or was a well known Chinese sage. Did he not play an important role in the formation of Christianity? None of these have been confirmed.

I choose to let the mystery remain, as there still circulate upon this Earth those who are pledged to harm him. I will simply state that Dr. Z. liveth in the present age in at least three separate human identities. They are living simultaneously but know each other not. All of them are extremely well hidden. One has served as a spiritual teacher but has long disappeared. His disciples search for him even now. Another has been a writer and a convict. The third prepares for his entry into the public awareness where he will cast a major influence, through the resonance of his voice alone, upon the affairs of this world on a spiritual plane.

Possibly only one of them is the real Dr. Z.—maybe all three. We definitely shall not discount the possibility that there are several more.

Any and all manifestations of Dr. Z. are free to complete their phase of service to the Earth and return Home.

Δ ΔΔ Δ ΔΔ Δ ΔΔ Δ

Father of the Sun and Mother of the Moon

These two, also known as the Ancient Ones, left Earth around the time of the completion of Atlantis when the Kingdom of AN disappeared from the physical plane. AN exists in a supra-dimensional reality on the White Star of SIAN within the universe which containeth a violet sky.

The Ancient Ones can be contacted through their reflected presence in our Sun and Moon as well as through our internal Sun and Moon.

Father-Sun and Mother-Moon watch over ANians still serving upon Earth. They have issued the Call to return many of their own back home to SIAN following this final embodiment. Thereafter the last traces of the Kingdom of AN shall depart the Earth forevermore. Thus shall the Great God AN complete its task of raising planet Earth from the realm of duality and seperation into conscious union with the One.

Δ ΔΔ Δ ΔΔ Δ ΔΔ Δ

The Hermit of the Crystal Mountain

I am no longer in human embodiment if indeed I ever was. Seek within for the Crystal Mountain. There I shall be found.

Δ ΔΔ Δ ΔΔ Δ ΔΔ Δ
Ma-Ah

She represents the Mother of all things. From her womb everything is brought to birth. Some say that she is the spirit of the Earth herself. Occasionally Ma-Ah will appear in dreams, visions, and meditations to those who are receptive to her energies. Great indeed are the teachings and initiations into the fount of her vast wisdom.

Presently she cries out to us for healing, for the pollution and desecration upon this planet are like unto wounds upon her body. At this time we should take little from her. Rather, we need to give her nourishment and healing utilizing the vortices of the fifth dimensional Light focus that are being activated upon her planetary body. As we transform and lighten, thus shall she be healed!

Eventually, after the Earth's purification has been completed, *(and ours as well)* it has been said that Ma-Ah shall shed her form as an ancient crone and reappear, renewed, as a beautiful young woman.

Δ ΔΔ Δ ΔΔ Δ ΔΔ Δ
Mu'Ra

She originated from the Sirian System and was the Last of the lineage of Mu'Ras. The original Mu'Ra was the true consort of Ra'Mu, *(also known as the Sun of Lemuria).* Together they were the founders of the Lemurian civilization. The spirit of Ra'Mu is ever present on this planet. He is one of the Masters of the dimensional vortex known as Mount Shasta, located in Northern California.

Concerning the final Mu'Ra found within the pages of our small history—after Altazar ended her earthly incarnation in TI-WA-KU, she finally returned to her galactic system. There she has undergone extensive restructurization procedures but remains stripped of her immense powers. We are pleased to report that Mu'Ra is reaching a new state of innocence. Her people, the four-fingered Sirians who originally colonized TI-WA-KU, have been severely reprimanded by the Interplanetary Council for abandoning her on Earth where she could cause harm unchecked.

Mu'Ra will not be permitted to travel again for some time until she achieves a certain level of purity and wisdom. When the final Mu'Ra develops to the degree where she becomes the embodiment of the first Mu'Ra, then the circle shall complete itself. On that day, she will rejoin Ra'Mu and their union shall produce a new star system where many advanced Sirians of the RA lineage will be sent as colonizers. And thus it shall begin anew.

Δ ΔΔ Δ ΔΔ Δ ΔΔ Δ

Namuani

This ancient woman has served on Earth since its first colonization, entering here with Aka-Capac. Namuani was closely connected with Alorah in the Temple of Oralin during the Golden Age of Atlantis when she and Soluna were twin sisters. In a later Atlantean epoch covered in this story, she was a musician famed throughout the continent.

Next Namuani was sent to colonize Egypt where she helped found the Temples of Anu in Heliopolis. In a yet later Egyptian lifetime as a male, she compiled what is now known as *The Papyrus of Ani*—part of the *Egyptian Book of the Dead*—leaving a record of the Egyptian Mysteries for future generations of mankind.

There were also numerous experiences in Peru with Aka-Capac, establishing the Inca civilization.

In the 16th century, Namuani appeared in India with her twin sister, another soul fragment, as temple dancers in Rajasthan. Being the only women ever admitted to this temple and initiated into this sacred form of movement, they were known far and wide for their beauty and grace. Through interconnected mudras, they could appear to disappear into each other in their invocations of feminine deities and shakti powers.

United long ago with Soluna into one being, Namuani lives among us today maintaining her conscious awareness of who she is, and serving as an example of the infusion of the Angelic sphere into the ancient energy patterns. A daughter of Sanat Kumara, Namuani/Soluna will be departing the Earth after this incarnation and has been reassigned to the Interplanetary Commission.

Δ ΔΔ Δ ΔΔ Δ ΔΔ Δ
Novasna
This pure spirit comes from the Angelic and starry realms. A true daughter of Alorah, Novasna has chosen to serve here as a representative of the Lorian Lineage.

After Novasna's experiences in Atlantis, she was sent by covered ship to Sumer. There she married a Sumerian King and encouraged the veneration of the Sky God Anu. *(Note here the connection with Heliopolis in Egypt.)*

Novasna has not had numerous lifetimes upon the Earth. Noteable among them were embodiments in ancient China with the Bodhisattva Kwan Yin and Namuani, as an Empress in Russia, in Arthurian Britian, and in Tibet. She also returned to the area of Sumer with Sargon of Akkadia, who was one of her great loves.

She lives in the present age in a secluded place with her mother. Novasna is a girl of starry eyes and radiant beauty. Maintaining recall of who she is and where she originates, she works on the spiritual plane as an adult. Novasna will return to Alorah after she completes her Higher Purpose on Earth.

Δ ΔΔ Δ ΔΔ Δ ΔΔ Δ

Og-Mora

Now, herein lies another story! His legend could well be termed *The ELegend of Og-Mora,* for was not this ELder of Lemuria one of the lineage of pure ELs of Arcturian descent? Alas, but no more pure ELs remain within Earth's gravitational field at this time. The distinguished Og-Mora was also one of the Og-Min.

Og-Mora experienced his ascension from the Earth plane at the moment of Lemuria's completion. Since then he was been working with the Interplanetary Council. Recently he has chosen to return here in the capacity of Witness. In order to do this, he had to combine his pure EL origin with another lineage and become what is termed a Hybrid-EL in order to survive within the denser frequency zones of the third dimension.

One of the personal reasons why Og-Mora chose to come here at this time was to locate Altazar and endeavor to awaken him. This older gentleman has traveled extensively throughout the world, observing it with fascination. After he feels that he has seen enough, Og-Mora will simply return from whence he came.

Δ ΔΔ Δ ΔΔ Δ ΔΔ Δ
Ptah

The Great God Ptah is the Lord of Life, the Master of Destiny, and the Creator of the World. He is the great-great-grandfather of the Gods, the Father of the Beginning, and the Creator of the egg of Sun and Moon. His staff combines the symbols of life, stability, and power. *Homage to you, O Great One!* We are indeed honored that you have chosen to appear within the pages of our humble legend.

Δ ΔΔ Δ ΔΔ Δ ΔΔ Δ
Seplik

Remember Seplik, he was the poor innocent from an outer Lemurian island who pierced the Mother Egg. Unspeakable has been his remorse over this severe misdeed since that fateful day deep in the heart of the volcano of Karak-oa.

Since then Seplik has lived numerous times as a Tibetan monk. He has also incarnated frequently among the Indian tribes of the Americas, tending to gravitate to life experiences which contain a simple physical environment close to nature.

Seplik still emanates a strong, physical vitality and tremendous courage. He has gained considerable knowledge, but has a simple, uncomplicated mind. Currently linked in service to the Tibetan Buddhist tradition as a respected Lama living in the West, Seplik has finally found inner peace and balance.

Δ ΔΔ Δ ΔΔ Δ ΔΔ Δ
Solana

This blessed one is beloved by both Angels and humans. Solana is the pure and dedicated spirit who departed Atlantis for Egypt with Namuani, whereupon they founded the College of Anu in the ancient city of Anu or Heliopolis. This settlement is referred to as ON in the Bible. A Tower of Light was created and the awareness of AN was brought into focus.

After Egypt, Solana appeared within many of those civilizations upon the planet wherein mankind made great steps forward in conscious evolution.

Solana originates from the starry realms of Og-Min. He was first sent to Earth as an Elohim. After a time, the Elohim were given the choice of returning to the celestial realms or remaining in service upon Earth. Solana chose to stay here. As with all the embodied Angels, it was necessary that they forget their true origin and descend into the limitations of matter in order to fully experience the physical plane. But as this lengthy cycle draws to its preordained conclusion, Solana and the others of his Angelic Brethren have begun to remember their Elohim heritage and are being activated into embodying their Angelic Presence. Once again, it shall truly be stated that the Angels walk among us.

And as I know that you are curious, I shall tell you. Solana is currently among us fulfilling his function as a multidimensional bridge, raising our level of consciousness into an accelerated awareness while searching for his beloved Twin Soul. *(Perhaps if he encounters our legend, it shall lead him to her.)* For do they not unite only at the beginnings and endings of major cycles?

This shall be their completion and final earthly union, for hence shall they depart together, rising into fullest flight on their Golden Wings of Light. And as they pass through the dimensional doorway which leadeth to the universe which contains the star system of SIAN, they shall merge until they are but the two wings of the same Angel. Ultimately this Angelic being shall unite with others of its star family, forming a new golden, white star of dazzling, radiant brilliance. And thus shall it truly complete itself and begin again.

△ △△ △ △△ △ △△ △

Soluna

Her original essence derives from the Starry-Angel realms. Before coming to this planet, Soluna served in the Sun-Arion System as the Keeper of Crystals. She lived in this embodiment for well over 2,000 years as measured in earthly time, dwelling within the Crystal Cave as a devoted and obedient servant, never once letting fall her duty. She has maintained that total devotion to her Higher Purpose.

Soluna is the main disciple on Earth of the Hermit of the Crystal Mountain. She is a linked spirit and has already merged with several of her essence fragments, including Namuani. They are as one today, and that one lives alone with her daughter Novasna near the Crystal Mountain holding and protecting the vision for the activation of the Crystal Mountain vortex.

Once Solana finds her they shall again manifest as the two tantric poles and fulfill their final Purpose together. Then they shall fly Homeward until they are called into action once again on a higher dimension.

Δ ΔΔ Δ ΔΔ Δ ΔΔ Δ
Vanel

He is a Master upon this planet in service to the lineage of AN, here solely by his choice, having been given the opportunity for his ascension long ago. Vanel has had numerous embodiments in Macedonia, Akkadia, Egypt, Peru and the Gobi. This ancient soul is strongly connected with Sanat Kumara.

In the present age, Vanel is once again a Master Musician currently living in Europe. Although well known and widely respected, he shuns public performances, preferring to create his unique form of musical magic in the privacy of his sound laboratory. Yes, Namuani knows his identity, but has yet to encounter him.

Vanel has served upon this planet with fullest dedication. He would indeed be astonished to realize the high degree of love and respect that is felt for him by the realms of mankind, Masters, Gods, Angels, and Starry Ones.

Δ ΔΔ Δ ΔΔ Δ ΔΔ Δ
Xeron

Xeron is a starry being from the Brotherhood of Og-Min, who is never required to incarnate into the limitations of the third dimension. The Og-Min manifest their wisdom and teachings on Earth through their initiates who have chosen to embody here as volunteer spirits. Xeron has not a physical body, but merely gathers to itself a collection of pure Light concentrated sufficiently to appear as a light body.

The Og-Min's greatest influence upon the destiny of

this planet was during the early colonization period of Lemuria and at a much later date through the Tibetan lineage. However, after the dispersion of the Tibetan teachings, those of the Brotherhood of the Og-Min can be found scattered freely among this planet.

The Call to Homecoming has sounded through a higher dimensional frequency, thus the Og-Min incarnate do rise into conscious activation and empowerment as they prepare to take their positions on the Homeward spiral.

Remember the refrain of the Og-Min:
There shall be No Down / No Return.

Δ ΔΔ Δ ΔΔ Δ ΔΔ Δ

As you can see, many human destinies hang in the balance, waiting for them to rise up into full conscious remembrance and activation. This process cannot be forced, for it requires a conscious decision on the part of each and every individual here incarnate. The doorway which stands open and beckoning in front of Altazar stands before many of you.

I know one thing for certain. *Altazar, I speak directly to you if ever you read these words.* Altazar, please know that the world needs you! Awaken and be your true shining self. If you and the others like you do not step forward into conscious manifestation of your higher selves and serve this planet in her time of greatest need, just who will do it?

Do you not realize that you are the elders, the planetary healers, the builders of the future? Each one of you is needed. Each and every one of you carries a special gift to the whole. Each one of you is crucial to the fulfillment of the Higher Purpose. Do not shirk your final duty. Do you not see that this is the reason why you were born? Please realize that all the experiences of your many lifetimes have led up to this point. They have prepared you fully so that you may fulfill your unique part in the Plan. All you need do is to step through the portal which stands before you and emerge into the embodiment of the radiant being that you are and always have been.

Come, I await you there. The Crystal Mountain awaits the ones who can activate its destiny. The time is right now or you would not be reading these words. And I must say unto you that we are given little time. We must come together now.

The Crystal Transmissions go forth unceasingly. But I ask you, who is there to listen? Please purify yourselves and open up the channels of receptivity to the higher frequency energies that beam down upon you.

ΔΔΔΔ*ΔΔΔΔ

My beloveds, back at the beginning of time, certain native and natural peoples were given the task of holding the world in balance. At various locations, scattered about the planet, vortices or pillars of Light were anchored deeply within the Earth. These ancient peoples, such as the Hopi, Tibetans, Ainu, and Dogon, have served their sacred Purpose well throughout the ages.

However, while initially each vortex was held and

maintained by a unified tribal group working together and sharing their common responsibility, such is no longer the case. Numerous of these tribal groups have disappeared from the face of the planet, making the weight greater on those who have remained. Even the groups who have managed to survive are no longer united in common purpose, indeed, many of them are beset by both internal and external pressures and strife. The pillars which hold this planet in balance have grown extremely precarious and crumbly indeed!

What must be done is that new energy vortices should be established and activated. They need to manifest upon this physical plane in order for this planet to survive. But I ask you, where are the dedicated ones ready to function as the anchors of the new vortices? See you not that this is an important part of your Purpose in being alive during this momentous time?

This is truly the final replay of the powerfully tragic lessons of fair Atlantis. The similarities are ever apparent. So are we going to sit back and passively allow the same pattern to repeat itself and let mankind make the same mistakes with even direr consequences? The ultimate test is before us.

ΔΔΔΔ*ΔΔΔΔ

The answers are within each of you. You need only be willing to ask the questions. The great teachers are still among us as they have been since the beginning of time. Simply look about you at Nature, look above at the Stars, and most importantly, look within yourself! Yes, it is as simple as that.

Please, dear ones, save your planet. Support each other with Love and Wisdom and work together, for you are all as unto the pillars of the Temple. Together—it will stand. Apart—it will fall.

Forget not the immense power of Love. Construct around the Earth a new grid or network of perfect, unconditional Love and Compassion. Remember that we are all in this together. There never has been and there never shall be any separation between any of us. We are all interconnected and interrelated, woven together in the garment of Oneness. By helping others, we help ourselves. By serving ourselves, we serve the whole.

ΔΔΔΔ*ΔΔΔΔ

It is important for you to realize that many of your ancient great ones shall be released from this plane once Earth's transition has been completed. I shall say unto them:

We want you to know how vast is our gratitude to all of you. Your service has been long and dedicated and your sacrifices great. Arise now, my dear ones, for the Sea of Oblivion has dried up and the Call to Return has issued forth. Your freedom beckons, almost within reach, yet ever elusive until you have danced your final Earthly dance. But does not the music begin to play? Choose your partners and step lively, for we shall dance with joyfulness.

Our gaze shall be on the Stars while we tap our feet lightly on the ground, tapping into the earth an infusion of celestial renewal.

And now is the time when you are Called upon to rise above the narrow spheres of personal karma. Gently free yourself from its grasp. Surrender thoroughly to your Higher Purpose and let go with love, thus you shall create ever more space within yourself for the entry of the supra-dimensional Light radiations.

Make haste in the development of your light bodies; they are a prerequisite for the Fifth Phase Transformational Activity. You must become fully activated, crystalline multidimensional beings, for you serve as the bridges for the Rising Golden Dawn.

Go forth and fulfill your final destinies with love, clarity and discernment. Know that as you acknowledge yourself as a pure vessel of the Divine Spirit, you shall be so empowered.

Freely send forth your crystal tipped arrows. They shall light your way, and therefore, enlighten the entire planetary body.

The spiral doth turn even now and if you have received the Call to Homecoming, you should prepare yourselves to take your proper position upon it. Yes, for truly the ancient star families are gathering together in order to affect their final mass ascension from this plane. Doubt this not!

ΔΔΔΔ*ΔΔΔΔ

After these ancient great ones have departed the Earth, remember that those of you who choose to remain must be prepared to fill their places. Hence there is no time to waste—no time to lose in anger, greed, confusion, self-indulgence or fear. A mighty transformation is unfolding. The spiral is turning. Are you ready to serve the Call of your True Self?

Remember dear ones, to lovingly accept yourselves, to end your denials, to merge into the highest octave of yourselves possible. Then simply be. Your bright, shining spirits shall be as glowing beacons of Light upon this reborn sphere—illuminating all with deep joy and profound peace.

Henceforth you shall be known as the Second Wave. You shall establish and maintain the Golden Dawn of a new, resplendent Golden Age.

Δ*Δ
ΔΔΔΔ*ΔΔΔΔ
Δ*Δ

Know that I watch over you with fullest Love. My blessings are with you always.

At last this Hermit need speak no longer. Slowly, gently, I return to the Silence . . . . .

ACKNOWLEDGEMENTS:

The writing of this book was a lengthy journey, taking over two years of my life, superimposing itself on my everyday realities. Sometimes, the words were winged and flew onto the paper effortlessly, requiring from me only a steady hand. Other times, it was more difficult. I had to overcome my fears, my self-doubts, my incomplete memories. And I personally lived through it all, experiencing all the wonder, devastation, sadness and poignance within THE LEGEND OF ALTAZAR

Now I wish to thank deeply those special beings who helped me forge ahead, encouraged me to continue, to complete this story. Some helped me proofread, others simply came through with enthusiasm, inspiration and loving support when it was most needed. With deep gratitude, I mention: Nova Sheppard, Josseph & Alice Rynear, Deirdre & Bill, James Bolen, Katie & Carl Keppler, Marian Starnes, Sherie Lewis, Doris Hartshorn, Elisabeth Kubler-Ross, Maria Quandt, José Argüelles, Riki Rutherford, Richard Mitchell, Nancy Sowanick, Hal Kramer, Kim Solga, Rolando Klein, Elara, Nion, Paloma, Gary Applegate, and Taoist Master Ni Hua Ching as well as Barbara Brown of Naturegraph. And most especially, I salute Solaris Antari and the Golden Solar Angels who helped me glide through on Wings of Light!

AVAILABLE FROM STAR-BORNE

Invoking Your Celestial Guardians – by Solara
Learn how to contact & embody your Golden Solar Angel.
This small, beloved book transforms lives. $6.95

The Legend of Altazar – A Fragment of the True History of Planet Earth – by the Hermit of the Crystal Mountain
A profoundly moving story of Atlantis, Lemuria & beyond,
which triggers the core of remembrance. It cannot be put
down or forgotten! $12.95

The Star-Borne: A Remembrance for the Awakened Ones – by Solara. A book too vast to attempt to describe, highly
recommended for all Star-Borne ones. $14.95

Audio Cassettes –The Celestial Message Series

Part One: The Angel You Truly Are
Guided meditations with Solara to contact your Golden
Solar Angel and find your name. Music by Etherium.
$10.00

Part Two: The Star That We Are
Guided meditations with Solara to unseal the Akashic
Records, send Divine Intervention and remember, release
& fly! Music by Etherium. $10.00

Part Three: Remembering Your Story
Guided meditations with Solara to remember your own
Divine Origins and Mission. $10.00

Part Four: Star Alignments
Brings in the Golden Light from Above and infuses your
body with stars, thus forming your Light Body. A simple,
yet profound transformative process. $10.00

Our Newsletter, *The Starry Messenger,* is available for
subscription at $25 per year.

Available from: Star-Borne Unlimited, Route 7, Box 191B
Charlottesville,VA 22901. (Please add $3.00 shipping for first item, .50
for each addt'l item.)